Computer Typing

IN THE SAME SERIES

Computer Typing

Made Simple Computerbooks

Betty and Warner Hutchinson

MADE SIMPLE
COMPUTER
BOOKS

HEINEMANN : London

Printed and bound in Great Britain
by Richard Clay (The Chaucer Press) Ltd, Bungay, Suffolk
for the publishers, William Heinemann Ltd,
10 Upper Grosvenor Street, London W1X 9PA

British Library Cataloguing in Publication Data

Hutchinson, Betty
   Computer typing made simple.—(Made simple
   books, ISSN 0265–0541)
   1. Electronic data processing—Keyboarding
   I. Title   II. Hutchinson, Warner   III. Series
   001.64′42   QA76.9.K48

ISBN 0–434–98404–3

Contents

Introduction

Computer Typing Made Simple is a guide for the person who owns—or has regular access to—a personal computer and who wants to use it more efficiently and with greater pleasure. A number of assumptions underlie the content and structure of this book:

1. You are interested in using your personal computer with greater ease, not in just learning how to type. In fact, you probably have very little interest in sitting down in front of a typewriter at all. Therefore, this book will make no direct reference to typewriter typing. You should think of this book as dealing with word and command entry, or "keyboarding," rather than "typing," but the term "typing" is so widespread that we have retained it.

2. You are not a typist or a secretary who wants to learn word processing. There are separate books on that subject. Here, however, we imagine that you are not primarily interested in generating heavy amounts of word output (unless you happen to be a writer and want to use your personal computer for manuscript preparation). In other words, we are not preparing you to be an office typist. Still, as you grow in proficiency in using your computer, you may generate more words—reports, summaries, proposals, letters—than at present you consider doing.

3. Our standard keyboard in this book is the IBM PC keyboard. We will discuss word and command manipulation functions using the IBM PC keyboard as our main model. However, in Chapter 12 we include a section on the keyboards of other major systems (Apple, DEC Rainbow, ACT Apricot, Tandy and so on), since these machines are also widely present in the marketplace. Most computers have similar functions. The names the manufacturers give these functions often vary, and the location and title of the keys that perform these functions often differ from system to system. If you have a system

other than the IBM PC and other than one also described in this book, you can readily translate our directions for use on your system by comparing functions and making the application to your system.

4. We use the QWERTY keyboard as our main approach to word and command entry. QWERTY is so named because the letters on the keyboard from the top left spell q-w-e-r-t-y. This system was adopted on manual typewriters early in the development of the typewriter; it was later used on electric typewriters; and it has since been put on the keyboards of most word processors and computers. Probably 99.9 per cent of all keyboards you will ever encounter are QWERTY keyboards. However, there is an alternative system of key arrangement called the Dvorak keyboard. It was designed in the 1930s and eventually named after its designer and chief proponent, August Dvorak. It provides a faster and easier option than the QWERTY keyboard and is becoming increasingly available for personal computers. Usually, though, it has to be specially ordered from a computer manufacturer, so if you are interested and your salesperson doesn't know about the availability of Dvorak keyboards, press the point. And since this book deals with the QWERTY keyboard, in Chapter 12 we have included considerable information about the Dvorak keyboard.

5. We also assume that you live a full, active life and that you don't want to attend "typing classes." Our book, designed for busy people, focuses on giving them familiarity with the keyboard itself as well as the main key functions needed to operate the computer. We assume you do not want to spend hours in intricate and onerous drill work in order to reach a prescribed level of accuracy and speed. We are not preparing you to pass a typing test. However, each time you sit in front of your screen doing your regular work, we urge you to spend a few extra minutes practising our simple drills. If you do so regularly, you will discover that your accuracy and speed will steadily increase to a level that will quite surprise you. Our aim is to give you greater pleasure in making your computer perform its tasks and to help you concentrate more on the tasks themselves than on the mechanics of getting the words and commands into the system.

And so, welcome to *Computer Typing Made Simple*. As you get into more and more interaction with your computer, we hope your family, friends, and colleagues will still see something of you from time to time!

1
The Electronic Word and Your Keyboard

As you sit in front of your screen, machine turned on, disks in the disk drives, and fingers poised above the keybord, it is useful to consider the nature of the electronic word and how that word and your keyboard are connected.

Words come in many forms.

Some are found on paper: a handwritten letter or memo, a typed report, or a printed book or magazine article. These words take on a kind of objective reality, since they physically exist on paper. We can go back to them time and again to review them and to search out levels of meaning they may contain. Because of our cultural reverence of sacred words and learned words, we tend to think of the written word as The Word. But still words are only representations of objects, ideas, and feelings that can also be thought about and talked about. Words on paper can be most useful (or else you would not have bought this book), but they are only one of a number of forms words can take.

Some words are ideas in your mind only; you never voice them or write them down. But you conceive them and use them in your thinking or your internal response about a situation. They can have a strong impact on you, even though no one else knows you ever thought them.

Some are voiced words. You speak them. Thoughtfully or spontaneously, in anger or in happiness, to influence or to direct or just to be companionable. They may be said person-to-person in a whisper or to millions of people over television.

1.1 THE ELECTRONIC WORD

A new form that is increasingly in widespread use is the "electronic word." These words are made up of tiny electrical currents. Each letter has its own pattern composed of electrical segments called "bits." Depending on the system, a letter can be made up of 8, 16, or 32 bits and can be expressed in an ASCII or EBCDIC patterns. In computerese, each unique combination of bits forms a "character." Some characters are letters, such as "a" or "A," or numbers, such as "3," or punctuation marks, such as "!," or spaces between words, or "returns" to end a paragraph, or tabs to indent a paragraph. Electronic text is made up of a character stream that contains letters, punctuation, spacing, and formatting characters.

These characters are created in your personal computer when you press a key on your keyboard. Your keyboard is wired to a series of integrated chips in your system's processing unit. When you press the "e" key, for instance, your system creates an electrical combination of bits that make up the combination for "e." The system displays that "e" on your screen and at the same time stores it in a temporary memory location. You can then add other characters after or in front of the "e"; you can move it to another location; or you can delete it. You can transfer the "e" from the temporary memory to a disk, where it is filed (stored) and can be recalled to your screen for further changing.

Once you have entered the word into your computer system and filed it on a disk, you have several options about further action with that word. You can call it back to the screen for editing; you can send an electronic "copy" of it to your printer for hard-copy reproduction; and you can send an electronic "copy" of it over the telephone to another computer system ("communications").

1.2 TYPING AND CHARACTERS

You enter the words by pressing the keys on your keyboard; this is called typing in this book. These words make up the content of your "document," that group of words—large or small in number—you have placed in one particular segment of your disk and have given a special name. You regain access to those words by calling up your document by that name from the disk. You can normally work on only one document at a time, although some systems will permit you to get data from other documents or to print one document while you are working on a different one.

But words made up of letters are not the only characters you enter into the system. You have to tell the system what to do with the words you are generating. You issue these commands to the system also by pressing keys on the keyboard. These commands may be accomplished by pressing a single key (for instance, "backspace" deletes the character to the left of the cursor), by a short group of letters followed by pressing an "execute" key, or by going into a "supershift," "code," or "control" mode and pressing a key. You type commands, just as you type words in your document. The cursor referred to in this paragraph is a movable, visible (often blinking) mark on the screen that indicates your current position. The cursor marks only one character (that is, one letter or one space or one punctuation mark or one command) at a time. Any commands you execute will occur at the cursor's location.

In *Computer Typing Made Simple*, we present both letters and commands in each chapter. As you become more and more familiar with entering letters into your system, you will be able to type both words and commands faster and with less direct attention to the mechanics of typing. We concentrate on the kinds of commands that enable you to arrange and rearrange the words in your documents. We do not deal with all functions of all possible commands that enable your computer to manipulate many fields of data. Those functions are described in manuals that accompany the various software programs you secure. For a simple illustration, we tell you about changing the gears in your car (how to type the words and commands), not where to travel in your car (the role of an ever-increasing array of software programs available from your manufacturer and retail outlets) or how specifically to get there (the role of the manual that accompanies your software).

We have seen the nature of the electronic word. Pressing keys on the keyboard is the method of entering, changing, manipulating, and communicating these words by means of commands; and typing is the fastest and easiest method of entering both words and commands. We will now look at the actual keys on your computer keyboard and their arrangement in general before we give you instructions and key-by-key practice in the succeeding chapters.

1.3 THE COMPUTER KEYBOARD

Your computer keyboard looks something like Figure 1 (remember, we are basing this book on the IBM PC keyboard); other sample keyboards appear in Chapter 12 (DEC Rainbow, Apple IIe, Tandy TRS 80, and ACT Apricot). If you have a different system, the keys

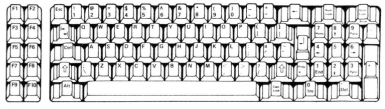

Figure 1

will be arranged slightly differently and some of them will be called by different names—but the general functions described here will apply to keys on your keyboard, whatever their arrangement. Your keyboard may have more or fewer keys, depending on the complexity of your system. Note that your keyboard is probably divided into functional sections.

Programmable Function Keys

The "programmable function" section is highlighted in Figure 2. On the IBM PC, there are ten programmable function keys, labelled "F1" to "F10." These keys perform different tasks, depending on the

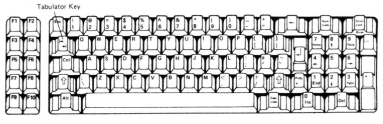

Figure 2

particular software program you have entered into your computer. Many manufacturers provide a template or a plastic label card to go around or above the programmable function keys. This contains a brief description or code of the function that the key performs for that particular software program. Templates or label cards change for each different software application. Your manual for the software program will describe the functions performed by each of the special function keys for the operation of that program. A sample of a template for the LOTUS™ 1-2-3 "spreadsheet" program used on an IBM PC keyboard is seen in Figure 3.

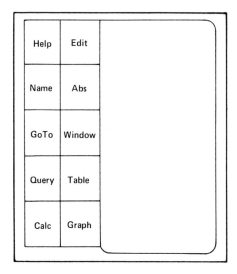

Figure 3

One of the benefits of touch typing is that you do not have to keep looking at the keys to know which one to strike. Our computer typing program in this book concentrates on typing without looking at the keys for the letters of the alphabet, plus several additional keys. However, we do not suggest you try to operate the special function keys without looking at them. As you become familiar with these keys and their use in your most often used software programs, you will soon press these most often used keys quite automatically, seldom looking at them. But when you use unfamiliar software programs and seldom used function keys, you have to look to make sure you press the right key to command the computer to perform the function you want.

Special Function Keys

Your computer has several special function keys that assist you in writing your programs, revising them, and running them out. These keys for the IBM PC are shown in Figure 4.

The "Esc" key is usually called the "escape" key. Its use is described in the manual for the particular software program you have loaded into your computer.

Many computer keyboards use the abbreviation "tab" for the tabulator key. When you set tab stops in the system, pressing this key will automatically advance your cursor to the next tab stop. This is an

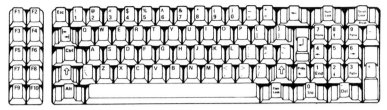

Figure 4

especially useful key for indenting paragraphs and for doing work that is laid out in columns, such as lists and financial reports.

The "Ctrl" key is a control key. This key is used in association with another key. By itself, it does not print a character. When used with some other key (described in software program manuals), it causes the computer to perform some function. Some manufacturers refer to this key as a "supershift"; but since that is a somewhat confusing term, most now call it by the term "control." This is one of the function keys you should begin to use without looking for it.

Most manufacturers actually label the "shift" key with the word "shift." There are two such keys on your keyboard; one is for your left-hand little finger, the other for your right-hand little finger. The usual function of the shift key is to create an uppercase or capital letter, or a symbol. The shift is used in association with another key. When the shift key is down, an alphabet letter will print in capitals rather than noncapital or lowercase letters. Where keys other than letters have two symbols, one above the other, the upper symbol will print when the shift is down and the key is pressed. The shift key works as follows:

The letter "a" appears on your screen if you press the "A" key.

If you press shift and hold it down while you press the "A" key, the capital letter "A" appears on your screen.

The number "7" appears on your screen, if you press the "7" key, which is also marked with an ampersand.

If you press "shift" and hold it down while you press the "7" key again, "&" appears on your screen.

The "Caps Lock" key, sometimes just called the "lock" key, puts the shift function into constant use until you disengage it. When the caps lock key is in use, ALL YOUR TYPING IS IN CAPS; IF YOU PRESS ANY NUMBER KEYS, THE RESULT WILL PROBABLY STILL BE THE NUMBERS. IN ORDER TO DISENGAGE THE CAPS LOCK KEY, JUST PRESS THE SHIFT KEY ONCE, and the cap-lock function is no longer in effect. (In some systems, you press the caps lock key a second time rather than shift to disengage the function.) The number keys still print numbers when the caps lock key is engaged; to get the symbols above the numbers, you have to press the shift key first even though the cap-lock function is on.

The "Alt" key is used in entering certain software command words. The software program manuals describe this use.

On many machines, the "backspace" key is called "backspace" or sometimes "delete." When it is pressed, it moves the cursor one character to the left (and remember, each space, punctuation mark, and command is also a character), and at the same time it deletes or erases that character. In most systems, you can hold the backspace key down and it will automatically keep moving back through the document and erasing until you release it. In some systems, you can automatically backspace/delete right back through your document to the beginning (or top) of it; with other systems, you can automatically backspace/delete only to the beginning of the particular line your cursor is in.

Some systems call the "enter" key the "return" key. It can serve a number of functions. It will move the cursor down to the beginning of the next line (in effect, beginning a new paragraph if you are writing a report or starting a new line of figures if you are preparing a financial statement). When you are giving instructions or commands to your computer, pressing this key after the command has been typed will enter the command into the system, and the system immediately "executes" the command. The enter or return key is another one of the function keys that you should learn how to use without looking at it. You press it with your right-hand little finger.

The next key down prints an asterisk (*) when pressed by itself. When pressed in conjunction with a shift, it causes the system to print out all the data that is displayed on the screen. This is the "PrtSc" or "print screen" function.

Ten-Key Number Pad

The IBM PC keyboard has a ten-key number pad for numeric entry, as well as having the numbers "1" to "0" across the top of the keyboard. Either set of number keys can be used to type in numbers. The ten-key pad is convenient when dealing with numeric calculations, the single-line numbers when typing in numbers along with words in running text. Many systems have both sets of number keys; many do not. Figure 5 shows the ten-key number pad.

When the "Num Lock" key is engaged, the ten-key pad works the

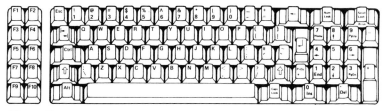

Figure 5

numbers "1" to "0" plus the "+" and "−" functions. You engage the num lock key by pressing it once. When you press it a second time, you disengage the key.

With the IBM PC, when the num lock key is disengaged, the keys in the ten-key pad control the cursor and perform other functions. One key moves the cursor up one line each time the key is pressed, and another moves the cursor down one line each time the key is pressed. A key moves the cursor to the right one character each time the key is pressed, and another moves the cursor one character to the left. Each of these keys will move the cursor automatically for as long as the cursor key is held down:

The "Home" key moves the cursor to the first character at the top of the screen when pressed. The "End" key moves the cursor to the last character on that line when the key is pressed (and depending on the software program, it may move the cursor to the last character in the entire document). The "Del" key deletes or erases the character where the cursor is positioned. When it does this, the text automatically moves in from the right to fill up the space that the deleted character had occupied. This key will continue to delete characters and "swallow" up your document if you keep the key depressed.

The "Ins" key is another one of the keys like caps lock and num lock that sets up or engages a mode of operation when the key is pressed once. In this case, it is the "insert mode," during which you can enter copy at the point where the cursor is located. Any copy that is already in the system to the right of the cursor will be moved automatically to the right of all the copy you enter while in the insert mode. To disengage the insert mode, simply press the insert key a second time, just as when disengaging from the caps lock or num lock keys.

The "PgUp" (page up) key moves your cursor up twenty-four lines (or the equivalent of one page), so you can view data you have entered but that does not at present appear on your screen. By repeated pressing of this key, you can "scroll" upward page by page toward the top or beginning of your document. The "PgDn" key performs the identical function as the page up key, only it moves the cursor down through the document page by page to the bottom (or end) of the document. The "Scroll Lock" key, when pressed simultaneously with the control key, allows you to halt the scrolling screen at any time. To continue, just press any other key.

The QWERTY Typing Keyboard

Now we look at the letter-and-number/symbol section of the keyboard. You use this section to enter words, symbols, numbers, and many commands and instructions. It is on this section of the keyboard that you do most of your typing; and therefore, it is this section that is the main subject of *Computer Typing Made Simple*. By going through this book, devoting some time regularly to the exercises and employing its method as you use your computer, you will learn to use this keyboard without looking at the keys and with ever-increasing accuracy and ease. This section of the keyboard is illustrated in Figure 6.

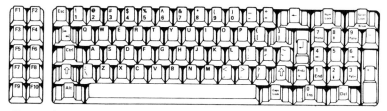

Figure 6

Note that the first six keys on the top line of the letters spell out QWERTY— a non-word; but this term is often used to identify this particular keyboard arrangement. The QWERTY arrangement was used early in the development of the typewriter and was soon adopted as *the* standard keyboard arrangement. Since millions of people have learned to type on this keyboard, computer companies have used the same arrangement as standard equipment on computers and word processors.

When the typewriter keyboard was originally designed, typewriters were cumbersome, manual machines. A typist's fingers were able to move much faster than the awkward machinery, and so the keyboard was designed to slow the typist up somewhat so as not to keep running ahead of the capacity of the machine to type. In more recent years, with electric and electronic keyboards, the speed of the equipment is able to match the fastest QWERTY typist with little difficulty.

The QWERTY keyboard has the following standard features:

1. The number keys run along the top line from "1" to "0." It is important to use a number "1" key for "one" instead of the letter "l" key, since these keys are wired to different electronic elements in the system, however much they may look alike when printed out. The same is true of the number "0" (zero) and the capital letter "O" (as in Oxford). On your screen, the number zero will have a slash through it, so you can tell it is a zero and not the letter "O." The number one has a distinct foot on which it stands, whereas the "l" does not have such a distinct foot, if it has one at all.
2. In the shift mode, these number keys produce symbols, such as "@," "%" or "&."
3. Punctuation marks are located in the lower right-hand corner of the keyboard, with the exception of parentheses (on the "9" and "0" keys).
4. The rest of the keys are the twenty-six letters of the alphabet. If the shift mode is engaged, you type the capital or uppercase form of the letter—"A"; and if the shift mode is not engaged, you type the lowercase form—"a."
5. The other keys you will use regularly in typing are the space bar, the return or enter key, the tab key, the shift key, the backspace key, and the caps lock key. Note that some of these keys are larger than the other keys, so you can more readily press them from any angle of the keyboard.

Up to now, the material presented in this book has been introductory in nature, aimed to give you an overall familiarisation with the keyboard and the functions of the varieties of keys that are there. From here on, you will find touch-typing instructions and short exercises. Follow the instructions and practise the exercises as you work at your keyboard. Before long, touch typing will become second nature.

2
Home Position

The very first skill you must learn is where to put your fingers for "home position." At first, this position might feel strange and you will have to look to be sure that your fingers are on the right keys, but in time it will feel quite natural to poise your fingers there before beginning to type.

The reason "home" is so important is that your fingers move up, down, and across from this primary position. If you are a key or a line off, your typing will end up being correct in that your fingers pressed all the keys in the proper locations but very wrong in that the keys of one hand are all one key off from what they should be. If your right hand is one key to the right of home, your typing will look like this: "upir tu½omg wo;; ;ppl ;ole tjos/."

2.1 THE HOME POSITION

To place your fingers correctly on home, your left little finger is on "a" and your right little finger on ";"; the rest of the fingers are on the keys that are right alongside, leaving the "g" and "h" keys uncovered. Your fingers are at a natural curl touching the keys with your palm about an inch to an inch and a half above the space bar. Don't lower the palms so low that you feel tension in your wrists or raise them so high that you feel awkward and strained in your shoulders. If you rest the heels of your palms on the keyboard base, your typing will be slow and awkward and your fingers will tire easily. Home position is illustrated in Figure 7.

As you sit in front of the keyboard with your fingers on the home keys, move your wrists up and down until the position feels the most comfortable. Depending on the level of your keyboard—whether it is on a table, a desk, or a terminal work station—and on the height and

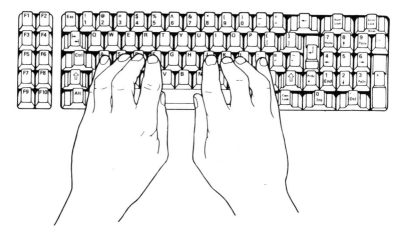

Figure 7

contour of your chair, you will have to adjust your posture until you feel at ease. Books that teach typing to people who will spend most of the day in front of a typewriter or a word processor stress the importance of posture and the use of the right kinds of desktop arrangements and back-support chairs. In this book, however, we are presuming that you are not going to spend the entire day entering words and commands into your computer and that you more likely are working on an office desk or a home table, not on a terminal work station. Therefore, find the position that fits your body and your work situation best and use that position as steadily as you can while you are using your keyboard.

Some keyboards are built right into the console that contains your screen; some keyboards are separate from the console, attached to it by a coiled cable. If your keyboard is separate, you have the option of moving it to slightly varying angles or even to a different level in order to find the location that is most comfortable for you. Some companies even advertise the "pleasure" that can be yours by putting the keyboard on your lap! To each his own. Experiment from time to time as you proceed through this book until you find the best possible combination.

You will also find that some jobs that require a great deal of input will require more discipline in maintaining firm posture, compared with other jobs in which you just bring a file up-to-date within a few minutes.

Now, with your fingers on the home keys and curled slightly but relaxed, and your body in a comfortable position behind the centre of the keyboard, you are ready to begin to type.

The first few exercises will seem very childish, because there are so few words you can put together from the limited number of letters in these early exercises. However, bear with us as we take you through them and soon you will sense the method in building blocks of frequently used parts of words as being basic to typing words and phrases.

Right-hand Fingers

With the first finger of your right hand, press the "j" key down lightly and quickly a number of times, watching the "j"s appear on your screen. Lift your finger quickly from the key and let it hover above the "j" key after each time you press it. Repeat this over and again until you sense you are pressing just hard enough to engage the key, but not so hard you have a feeling of pounding or pushing it. Your key makes an electrical connection, which completes an electronic circuit that enters your letter into the system. You do not have to perform any heavy mechanical action. So practise at being quick, precise, and light enough in touch to make the electrical connections with the least amount of effort on your part. Since each manufacturer's keyboard has a slightly different feel, and indeed even each keyboard on the same machine model has its own unique feel, practise on your keyboard.

Do the "k" with your second finger,

kkkkkkkkkkkkkkk

the "l" with your third finger,

llllllllllllll

and the ";" with your little finger—this will feel quite awkward at first.

;;;;;;;;;;;;;;;

Concentrate on moving your little finger up and down, not your entire hand from the wrist.

Left-hand Fingers

Give your right hand a rest and continue the same exercise with your left hand.

Do the "f" with your first finger,

ffffffffffffff

the "d" with your second finger,

dddddddddddddd

the "s" with your third finger,

ssssssssssssss

and finally, the "a" with your little finger.

aaaaaaaaaaaaaa

If you are right-handed, the "a" will seem the most awkward of all at first, but in no time you'll be used to it.

Now add the space bar to your repertory. Use *only* your right thumb to press the space bar. (Your left thumb has a free ride in all your typing.) Press "f" and the space bar, using the left first finger and the right thumb, one after the other several times:

f f f f f f f f f f

Try the "d" and space,

d d d d d d d d d

the "s" and space:

s s s s s s s s s

and the "a" and space:

a a a a a a a a a a

That group is easy since you are alternating hands.

The next group calls for the use of right-hand fingers and your right-hand thumb.

Using your right first finger and your right thumb, do the "j" and space,

j j j j j j j j j j

then the "k" and space,

k k k k k k k k k

the "l" and space,

l l l l l l l l l l

and the ";" and space.

; ; ; ; ; ; ; ; ; ;

Notice how much is precise, lightly stroking finger action. You will also have noted by now that your computer automatically drops to the next line when you have filled up a line with characters.

There is no need to signal the end of each line by pressing the return or the enter key. If fact, if you did that, you would only be creating problems in formatting your document. Let the computer take care of line endings when you are typing straight copy.

Both Right-hand and Left-hand Fingers

Combine your right-hand and left-hand keys with spacing by working your way in from the little finger:

asdf ;lkj asdf ;lkj asdf ;lkj asdf ;lkj

Try to develop a rhythm as you do it in patterns of four:

asdf ;lkj asdf ;lkj

The main point for now is not to type anything that makes any sense, but to feel the pattern of using all four fingers of each hand, with the right thumb coming in from time to time to provide spacing.

After a few more, try going the other way—from the first finger out:

fdsa jkl; fdsa jkl; fdsa jkl;

This will slow you down a bit since it is not as "normal" as working inward from the little finger. Don't worry about speed at this point. Concentrate on an ease of rhythm in getting your fingers to do something you have not trained them to do in such a concentrated space.

As you do these exercises, watch the screen, not your fingers. Don't be concerned about the mistakes (misstrikes) that show up on your screen.

There are only a limited number of real words that you can put together using just the keys of the home position on a QWERTY keyboard. "As" is the most obvious one. Try it a few times and you will be typing your first word without looking at the keyboard:

as as as as as as as

Since you are using the two least used fingers of your left hand, it will probably feel awkward at first if you are right-handed.

Add a letter and blend some left-hand/right-hand combinations:

lad lad lad lad

Try:

lass lass lass lass

Other real words call for precise left-hand use alone. Try them, but do so slowly, getting used to the location of the keys, your fingers, and the skill of moving your fingers in different sequences:

dad dad dad dad

Now try:

fad fad fad dad lad fad mass as

If you are having trouble feeling at ease with this finger movement, try:

sad sad sad sad

That word will probably be the toughest of all, since you are reversing the movement from the centre outward in "s a d."

Don't cut corners and look at the keyboard as you type these words. If you make mistakes, just leave them. (They'll vanish forever when you turn your system off—unless you want to "file" this first practice document and keep it as a memento.) At this moment, you could surely type these simple words faster using two fingers and your eyes, but train yourself as you are learning to touch-type on your computer to use the proper finger to press the proper key and to do so without watching what you are doing. Watch only the screen. Before long, your left-hand little finger will be "a" in the home position. In a very short while, you will not have to think where it is. You'll think "a" and your left-hand little finger will respond.

2.2 FUNCTIONS

In each chapter, there is a special section on computer functions as they relate to typing. Use of function keys will enable you to better deal with words and commands. For some of the functions, we recommend learning how to touch-type in using those keys, because you will use them often and the keys are convenient for touch typing. For other functions, we suggest you look regularly at the keyboard to find and use the key.

Backspace and Delete

The first function is to "erase" or delete a character. We chose this first because we all make mistakes frequently when entering words and commands.

On the IBM PC and on most computers, the proper key to delete a mistyped character is located two lines up from the home line and is next to the "=" key. It may be called "backspace" or be an arrow pointing to the left. This is a touch-type key.

The proper finger to use is your right little finger. From home, over the ";" key, lift your little finger up and right to reach the backspace key and strike it quickly and firmly. The character to the left of your cursor will disappear from the screen. You have removed it from the system; you can leave the result as you see it on the screen, or you can add in any character or number of characters you want in its place.

At first, you have to look when you move your finger up to the backspace key to make sure you're getting to the right one. But keep practising the move until you "feel" the proper direction and distance to find it with your little finger without watching your hand. Each time after you press the backspace key, return your finger to the home position. Very lightly touch your home keys to assure yourself that you are really there. Don't try to move just the finger by itself; your wrist and hand can drift in that direction and then help pull the finger back to home again.

Try some

> as fad lad sad lass

words again. Watch the screen—not your fingers. When you make a mistake, like "laas" instead of "lass," delete the "as"; then put the right letters in without looking at the keys.

In time you'll be able to correct your mistakes as you type along almost as fast as you entered them in the first place. You will come to "feel" when you have pressed the wrong key for a letter ("laas" for "lass"), and you will have made the correction almost before you are consciously aware of having done so. But for now, concentrate on using the little finger for the backspacing/deleting task.

Move Cursor

The second function is to move your cursor to where you want to enter or correct words. At the beginning, we do not suggest you use touch-typing methods for cursor manipulation. First, there is no standard location of the cursor keys on computer keyboards. As you get used to using the cursor location keys on your keyboard, you may very well develop your own touch-typing routine that enables you to move the cursor with minimum visual checking to make sure you're on the proper key.

But for now, find those keys that have the up-and-down and side-to-side arrows. Press them until you get a good feel for the way they move the cursor through your document. Try pressing them in conjunction with pressing the control key. Usually the control key is on the left-hand side of your keyboard, and the cursor keys are somewhere on the right-hand side. Practise pressing the control key with your left-hand little finger while you press a cursor key with one of your right-hnd fingers. You will probably find that the control and cursor key combination moves your cursor all the way in the direction of the arrow, not just one character or one line at a time. It may be a line, a page, or the entire document, depending on your system.

Now you can position your cursor to the proper place in your document to add or delete characters or words. Position your cursor to the right of a character you want to delete, and then press the backspace key. Position your cursor where you want to enter a character or space, and press the appropriate key or the space bar.

Shift

The third function is use of the shift keys. Note that there are two such keys on the bottom line of the keyboard. These keys are pressed by the left or right little finger. Try the motion of moving down and out from the home position, with the little finger leading the rest of the hand. Try it alternately several times, left then right, then left then right, going back to home each time. You'll have to look at first; then try it without looking until you have the feel of the distance and direction.

You use the left little finger on the shift key when you want to make a capital letter or symbol with one of the keys that are "right-hand keys." Conversely, you use the right little finger on the shift key to make a capital letter or symbol with a "left-hand key." Try it, slowly at first to get the idea of the coordination:

Left little finger: down and out to shift; right third finger: press the "l" key— producing a capital "L"; now go back to home and type "a" (left little finger) and "d" (left second finger)—"Lad."

Try it a few times to get the rhythm of the movement:

Lad Lad Lad Lad Lad

Now reverse the process with the capital letters and use the right little finger shift to produce:

Sad; Sad; Sad; Sad;

or

Fad; Fad; Fad;

or

Dad; Dad; Dad;

Caps Lock

And the last position for this chapter is the caps lock key. Press caps lock and listen for it to engage with a slight clicking sound. On some keyboards the shift keys will appear to be depressed when you engage the caps lock key (depending on your keyboard). Type:

LAD: LAD: LAD: SAD: DAD: FAD

This cap-lock feature is especially useful if you are typing a report and want section headings or titles to be all caps. It is not unusual to forget that you have engaged the cap-lock function and to proceed to type the regular text in caps. If you're watching your screen, you see this take place within a few characters, backspace to delete the letters in caps, then disengage the caps lock key by pressing it once (the shift keys will then return to their normal position if your keyboard has depressed them during the time caps lock was engaged), and proceed to type normally.

In Chapter 2 you have learned home position. Be sure to return your fingers to the home position whenever you move them to a different line to press a key. It is from the home position that you will come to feel the right amount of distance and direction to move a finger to press a key other than your home keys. You have also learned four essential functions: (1) backspacing and deleting; (2) moving your cursor to the position you want; (3) shifting keys in order to get capitals and symbols; and (4) using the caps lock in order to get an entire word or line in caps. And you have begun to operate your primary function keys (backspace-and-delete and shift) by touch together with the keys of your home position.

When you are away from the keyboard, pretend you have a keyboard in front of you and practise finding the keys of the home position with the correct finger:

a s d f   j k l ;

Visualize them in your mind and be sure to use the correct finger to press them. You will find this mental keying will prove beneficial when you are back in front of the keyboard again.

3
New Keys: ec i,

You will now begin using keys other than those on the home position line. Because the human body tends to favour a pattern of symmetry, we will concentrate in this chapter on the second finger of both the right and left hands. The horizontal lines on your keyboard are clear enough—they go straight across from one side of the keyboard to the other. The vertical lines, however, slant slightly to the left when reaching for a key above the home line and slightly to the right when reaching for a key below the home line. The keys for the second finger are the darkened ones in Figure 8.

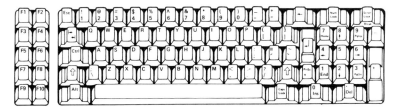

Figure 8

3.1 SECOND FINGER KEYS

Your home position for the second fingers are: left second finger "d"; right second finger "k." Place your fingers on home, and then raise just your left second finger to "e" and press the key, then return your finger to home. On your keyboard the letter "e" is used more often than any other letter in the alphabet.

Now do the same with your right second finger to press the "i" key. You now have three of the five vowels at your command: "a," "e," and "i."

Try some words by combining elements in your home position and these two new keys:

> life life life
> fife fife fife
> side side side
> lade lade lade
> like like like
> Jake Jake Jake
> sake sake sake

Put in the punctuation marks that you have already learned on your home row:

> life; Jake: like; side: sake;

The pseudonym of a famous Scottish author was Saki:

> Saki Saki Saki

And sometimes if you have dinner at a Japanese restaurant, you might try some sake:

> sake sake sake

Having moved the second fingers up one line and slightly to the left, now try moving them down one line and slightly to the right: Move the right second finger to "," and the left second finger to "c."

Here are some words that connect the "c" and "," to the home keys:

> flack flack flack
> sack sack sack
> lack lack lack
> fad, dad, sad,
> fad, dad, sad,
> lad, Jack, Jack

And here are some that use the home keys and the keys where the second fingers go both up and down:

> lick, flick, Dick,
> jack, Jack,

local, less, Ali,
sell, Sid,
Jack likes Jackie;
Sid likes Jackie:
Jackie likes Dale;
Dale likes Lisa;
Lisa likes Jack

Each time your second finger moves up or down to press a key, be sure to return it to the home key again so it is ready to strike the home key or to move away again from the home position for one of its other keys.

Now try some harder combinations that use one finger on all three lines for the same word:

cede cede cede
secede secede secede secede

And now from the bottom line to the top line:

dice dice
lice lice
slice slice slice
lace lace
face face

And now some more intricate finger movements:

ease ease ease ease ease ease ease
lease lease lease lease lease lease
lies lies lies lies lies lies lies
flies flies flies flies flies flies
dies dies dies dies dies dies dies
said said said said said said said
dais dais dais dais dais dais dais
leis leis leis leis leis leis leis
case case case case case case case
class class class class class class
jackal jackal jackal jackal jackal
jade jade jade jade jade jade jade
jell jell jell jell jell jell jell
Jeff Jeff Jeff Jeff Jeff Jeff Jeff
kale kale kale kale kale kale kale
kail kail kail kail kail kail kail
keel keel keel keel keel keel keel

leak leak leak leak leak leak leak
kick kick kick kick kick kick kick
lick lick lick lick lick lick lick
kids kids kids kids kids kids kids
skids skids skids skids skids skids
Klee Klee Klee Klee Klee Klee Klee
sled sled sled sled sled sled sled
dales dales dales dales dales dales
lads lads lads lads lads lads lads

Type these combinations until you begin to feel more at ease with moving your fingers in various combinations to produce the results you want. Don't look at your keyboard while you do this. Right now you are focusing on finger control and a steady rhythm more than on letter-perfect accuracy. As you develop a flow in your finger control, accuracy will increasingly come of its own.

Note that the shift mode used with the "," produces a "<" (an open "vee" bracket), and the shift mode used with the "." produces a ">" (a closed "vee" bracket). If you are typing scientific, mathematical, or statistical copy, you can use these symbols for "less than" (<) or "greater than" (>). You can combine them with an underline to create symbols that mean "less than or equal to" (≤) or "greater than or equal to" (≥). And you can put a vertical line through them to produce symbols that mean "is not less than" (≮) or "not greater than" (≯). But most often these "vee" brackets are used in entering data in a computer program. Depending on the software, the computer will treat data within the bracket differently from the same data entered alone.

3.2 FUNCTIONS

Block Move

The only function we will discuss in this chapter is the capability your computer has—with an appropriate software program—to move a block of text from one place to another. Word-processing programs have this function. Indeed it is one of their most useful enhancements for people who use their computers to write—whether it be correspondence, reports, articles, or books. Every writer looks over the first draft and then starts to think of better ways to organize the material. First, changes should be made for certain words. There is often a better word than the one you first chose. You rummage through your mind for just the right word. If you don't find it there, you try dictionaries, synonym books, or a thesaurus. One lead moves you to another, and finally you have the right word. Putting it into your document is easy—you just delete the word you don't want and type in the word you do want. And the computer rearranges your document around the change.

But the more you look at what you have written—now that you've got the best words in—the more readily you see that if you changed the order of some of your phrases, or your sentences, or even some of your paragraphs, the impact on the reader would be stronger and the communication of your ideas would be clearer. And moving blocks of text around from one place to another in your computer is easy. You can move a single character and as many as 2,000 characters, depending on system and its memory.

We cannot here tell you just which keys to press to accomplish this task, since that depends on your system and the software program you are using. But the directions will be very clear in your software manual. For the IBM PC using an "EasyWriter" word-processing program, for instance, you move your cursor to the beginning of the block of text you want to move. Then you press the "insert" key to enter the insert mode. Then you press the "F8" (one of the function keys), which in the EasyWriter program is programmed to perform this function. You then move your cursor to the end of the block of text you want to move and press the "F8" key again. You will see on the screen when you press the "F8" key that the block of text has been marked off from the rest of the document. Now you press the "control" key and hold it down while you press the "C" key. When you do this, the system removes the text from your document (while you watch it disappear) and places it in the system's buffer or temporary memory. Then you move your cursor to the location where you want to place the block of text. You press the "F3" key, which opens up some space into which the block of text can be inserted. Again you press and hold the "control" key and press the "G" key. When you do this, the system removes the text from the temporary memory and reinserts it into this new location in your document.

If you are using some other word-processing program, such as WordStar, Super Script, Apple Writer, Atari Writer, or Bank Street Writer, the actual commands (the keys you press to perform the function and the sequence in which you press them) will be different from those just described for the IBM PC/EasyWriter combination.

But the principle (or "logic") is the same. You block out the text you want to move, instruct your system to store it temporarily in the system's buffer memory, locate the place where you want to reinsert the block of text, and instruct your system to "dump" it from the buffer memory back into your document.

Block Copy and Block Delete

If your system has the capability of moving blocks of text (and virtually all systems—that is, hardware and software combinations—do), then it can also probably perform some additional functions with the block of text you have set apart. It can copy the block elsewhere, which means it can duplicate the block of text at some other location in the same document or even in a different document, without removing it from its original location. It can also delete the block all at once, rather than your having to delete it character by character.

In each instance, you define the block of text you want to act on and then you follow the instructions in your software manual to move it elsewhere, copy it elsewhere, delete it, or even save it for the time being to be used later on. "Saving" it usually requires filing it somewhere so you will have access to it in the future.

4
New Keys: rv um

4.1 FIRST FINGER KEYS

Having grown used to moving your second finger up and down one line at a slight angle, now you will use your first fingers. Figure 9 shows these keys.

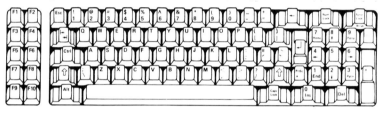

Figure 9

Try it for a few times to get used to the distance and location:

fr fr fr fr fr fr fr fr fr fr fr fr
rf rf rf rf rf rf rf rf rf rf rf rf rf rf
fr rf fr rf fr rf fr rf fr rf fr rf fr rf
ju ju ju ju ju ju ju ju ju ju ju ju
uj uj uj uj uj uj uj uj uj uj uj uj uj

The right-hand movement is a bit more difficult since you have to use the right thumb for the spaces as well as the right first finger for the letters. Try some more moving your fingers up:

frf frf frf frf frf frf frf frf frf frf
rfr rfr rfr rfr rfr rfr rfr rfr rfr rfr
juj juj juj juj juj juj juj juj juj juj
ju uj ju uj ju uj ju uj ju uj ju uj

and then down:

```
fv fv fv fv fv fv fv fv fv fv fv fv fv
vf vf vf vf vf vf vf vf vf vf vf vf
jm jm jm jm jm jm jm jm jm jm jm jm jm
mj mj mj mj mj mj mj mj mj mj mj mj mj
jmj jmj jmj jmj jmj jmj jmj jmj jmj
mjm mjm mjm mjm mjm mjm mjm mjm mjm mjm
fvf fvf fvf fvf fvf fvf fvf fvf fvf fvf
vfv vfv vfv vfv vfv vfv vfv vfv vfv
```

Try both up and down (remember, for now you are just getting used to the finger movement and the location of the keys in relation to home position). Look away from the keys and at the screen as much as you can and think the letters as you press the keys:

```
frfv frfv frfv frfv frfv frfv frfv frfv
rfv rfv rfv rfv rfv rfv rfv rfv rfv
vf rf vf rf vf rf vf rf vf rf vf rf
rv vr rv vr rv vr rv vr rv vr rv vr
jujm jujm jujm jujm jujm jujm jujm jujm jujm
mum mum mum mum mum mum mum mum mum
umu umu umu umu umu umu umu umu umu umu
mj jm mj jm mj jm mj jm mj jm mj jm
um mu um mu um mu um mu um mu um mu um mu
```

You now have four of the five vowels at your disposal. Think through where they are and press them in sequence through the alphabet, and then backward:

```
aeiu aeiu aeiu uiea uiea aeiu uiea
```

And you have several consonants at your disposal. In the order of the alphabet, they are:

```
cdfjklmrsv
```

Looking at them on the screen, type them out a few times, thinking through which finger to use on which line to produce the desired letter:

```
cdfjklmrsv cdfjklmrsv cdfjklmrsv cdfjklmrsv
vsrmlkjfde vsrmlkjfde vsrmlkjfde vsrmlkjfde
```

Don't worry if you have to pause a bit to remember which finger to use on which line for which key. This is an entirely new pattern of coordinating your eyes, mind, and fingers. Take your time as you feel your way around the keyboard.

Now add some of the four vowels and make some words on the screen. Start with some "re" words, since you'll use a lot of these in everyday usage:

> reuse reuse reuse release release release
> resend resend resend relieve relieve relieve
> rekiss refind refind refind recase recase

Some "er" words:

> laser laser laser fiercer fiercer fiercer
> sadder sadder sadder lamer lamer lamer
> vermicelli vermicelli verse verse versifier

Here are some words that use a whole range of the vowels and consonants you now know how to use:

rum rum rum radar radar radar frame frame frame Miss Jamie Summers Mr. James Keane Mr. James Keane Kursk Mr. James Keane calls Kursk, as is Miss Jane Summers relives a kiss Mr. Keane dared as safe leave leave relieve relieve receive receive keel keel leak lead read red readier seamier seam sieve sieve sear seer clear clearer seek seek seem seam seem seed seduce seduce seclude seclude secede suede suede suffer surf surface surface surf survive survival juridical juridical juicier juju Julius Jesse James Jerusalem eider elder adder madder ladder seller lesser rue due slue clue

Note how your fingers begin to pick out familiar combinations of letters (that is, combinations of finger movements) and put them together in sequence to form parts of words. Such combinations you have encountered so far include:

> cl er re ei se es ier all is ea nd

As you proceed in typing you will find certain combinations come easy to you. Use them as building blocks in putting together words as you type.

4.2 FUNCTIONS

In order to print words on a page, it is necessary to set the right-hand and left-hand margins, as well as the top and bottom margins, for your page. If you are using a word-processing program, there are margin instructions in your manual. Again, we will set forth the sequence of steps for the IBM PC/EasyWriter program. The names of the steps and the sequence of keys will differ somewhat in your program, but the principle will be similar.

Top and Bottom Margins

There is a basic pattern to keep in mind when setting margins. Think of a sheet of paper, a label, or an envelope as having an invisible grid. The number of lines to the grid depends on some choices you make and feed into your computer.

Let's use an $8\frac{1}{4}'' \times 11\frac{3}{4}''$ sheet of paper—the most commonly used size (A4)—as an example. Since eventually you will print the words you enter into the system onto that sheet of paper, you need to enter certain pieces of information to tell the printer where you want the printing to appear.

The first step is to determine how many lines of printing could appear on the paper. Most programs are set to print out copy at six lines per inch (6 LPI). This means there could be seventy lines of printing on a sheet of paper eleven $11\frac{3}{4}$ inches long. If you are using a 6 LPI setting, your horizontal grid consists of seventy lines, although it is most unusual to try to fill up a sheet with seventy lines of printing. You normally leave a top and bottom margin. If you want a one-inch margin on the top, you tell your computer to begin printing on line 7 (six lines—or one inch—are left blank, giving you the one-inch margin you wanted). And if you want an inch-and-a-half margin at the bottom, you tell your computer that line 61 is your last line to print. Lines 62–70 (a total of nine lines) are left unprinted, providing you with your desired margin.

It may be that you are printing the first page with a letterhead of a two-page letter. The second page is to be printed on blank paper. The lines 7–61 setup is fine for the second sheet, but if you used it on the first sheet, you would overprint part of your letterhead. When you measure your letterhead, you find that you want to start printing just after the two-and-a-half-inch mark. The two-and-a-half inches take up fifteen lines, so you will start the first page on line 16, the second page on line 7.

Many programs and printer hardware have the capability of printing at eight lines per inch (8 LPI) as well as 6 LPI. If you choose to use this option, you have to tell the machine that you want to do so. Then you have to recalculate your horizontal grid. There are now ninety-four lines of possible printing instead of seventy. One inch is eight lines, so you would start on line 9 if you wanted a one-inch top margin, and on line 21 if you wanted a two-and-a-half-inch top margin. You would print your last line on line 82 if you wanted to leave an inch-and-a-half margin on the bottom.

Think through the grid, and then instruct your system to print where within the grid you want.

Double Spacing

Your system probably has the option of double spacing, as well as having single spacing. For most correspondence you will most likely use single spacing (each line is printed), but for reports or drafts of letters or books, or for final pages of books or articles to be submitted to a publisher, you will want to double-space. Here there is a line of space between each line of printing. Your system will automatically insert that line of space when printing, if you so instruct the system when setting up the printing directions. With many word processing programs you will not, however, see that line of space between each line of printing when you look at the document on your screen.

When you set your top and bottom margins for double-spaced printing you need to take those extra lines of space into account when thinking through your grid. You will now have only thirty-five lines of actual printing possible on the page: Line 1 is possible print; line 2 is space; line 3 is possible print (the second line of printing); line 4 is space; line 5 is possible print (the third line of printing); and so on. On a 6 LPI setting (the one you will normally use), you start printing on line 4. There are three lines of space added to lines 1, 2, and 3; therefore, line 4 is the next line after one inch of space (line 1, line of space, line 2, line of space, line 3, line of space, or six lines altogether). Your last line of printing will be line 31. There will be twenty-eight lines of actual printing on your page (remember lines 1, 2, and 3 are part of your top margin). Lines 32, 33, 34, and 35 are part of your bottom margin (remember that after each line your printer will add a line of space). You have had to calculate the line of space after each line that could be printed as part of your grasp of the way the grid fits on your paper. (Compare Figures 10 and 11.)

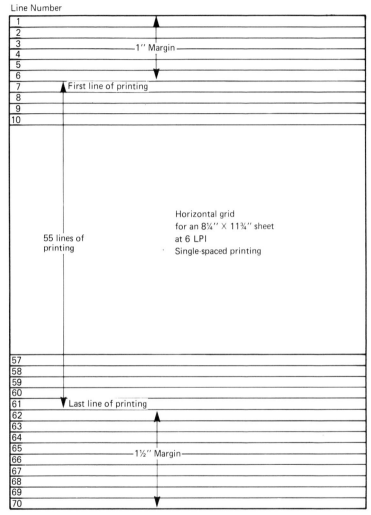

Figure 10

Side Margins

You also have to calculate the vertical grid. Most computers can print a larger-sized typeface of ten characters per inch (10 CPI) (often called "pica" type) or a smaller-sized typeface of twelve characters per inch

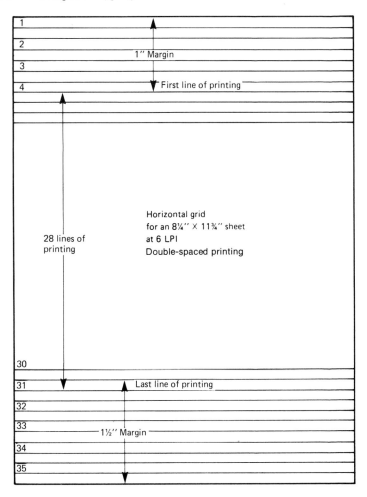

Figure 11

(12 CPI) (often called "elite" type). A few sophisticated program and hardware combinations can print an even smaller typeface of fifteen characters per inch (15 CPI). And some can print with proportional spacing. In 10-, 12-, and 15-CPI printing, each character takes up the same amount of horizontal space, whether it is an "m" or a "w," or an "i" or a "t." In proportional spacing, the amount of space taken by a character depends on the shape of the character: The "m" is much wider than the "l"; the "w" is wider than the "g," which in turn is wider than the "r." The computer needs to do a great deal of arithmetic

computation of units of space in order to instruct the printhead on how far to move from character to character when printing proportionally. Therefore, most lower powered computers do not have this extra capability as a part of their normal operations.

For 12-CPI Characters

Let us assume that your printer prints a 12-CPI character. It may be a dot matrix printer, so your character will be a combination of tiny dots in the shape of the character. The better the quality of printer the closer the dots will be to each other, the more dots there will be to a character, and the sharper the letter will appear. Even the best dot matrix printer, however, produces a character that seems slightly blurred, due to the spaces between parts of the dots no matter how close they are. An impact printer, using either a round "golf ball," a "thimble" printing element, or a "daisywheel"-spoked printwheel produces sharply outlined characters, similar to those of a typewriter. A highly defined dot matrix character takes longer to produce than one made up of a few dots; and an impact printer usually runs at a slower speed than a dot matrix printer. Most computer systems have the capability of having their components upgraded, so you can improve the quality of your printout when you wish to do so by changing the printer. Regardless of whether your printer is a dot matrix or an impact printer, our assumption right now is that it prints at 12 CPI.

You are, therefore, theoretically able to print 99 characters across an $8\frac{1}{4}''$ sheet of paper (8.25 inches $\times$ 12 CPI) = 99 characters). But rarely would you want to print right across the entire page. You may want to have a margin of one inch on the left-hand side of the sheet and a one-and-a-half-inch margin on the right-hand side. Your vertical grid has 99 spaces. You would start printing on space 13, leaving the first twelve spaces blank for your margin. Your last space on the right for printing would be 81, leaving spaces 82–99 (eighteen spaces) as the inch-and-a-half right-hand margin.

Call up the proper menu for setting margins and set in a 13/81 combination. This permits you to type up to sixty-nine characters per line ($5\frac{3}{4}$ inches of characters + a 1 inch left margin + a $1\frac{1}{2}$-inch right margin = $8\frac{1}{4}$ inches). If you later decide to widen your margins to $1\frac{1}{2}$ inches on the left and 2 inches on the right, you merely recalculate your margin settings (19/75 are the new settings), put them in at the beginning of your document, and (depending upon the program you are using) run your cursor through the document. The document will reshape itself around these new settings without your having to reset each line.

Use of the Grid

By using this grid concept you may place type at any place you want on the sheet of paper. Calculate the grid location: how many lines down from the top? How many spaces in from the left? Move your cursor down to the line and across to the space, and type in your entry. When you print it out, it will appear on the sheet of paper just where you wanted it.

You can also place addresses or titles on envelopes or labels by using the same grid approach. However, instead of being an 8¼″ × 11¾″ sheet, your envelope (a no. 10) is probably 4″ × 9½″. The grid pattern is the same (6 LPI and 12 CPI) but the size of the field for the grid is smaller.

Figure 12 gives you a picture of the vertical grid, with your margins set for the 13/81 left-and-right combination. This grid is based on a twelve-pitch line, using 8¼″ × 11¾″ sheets of paper.

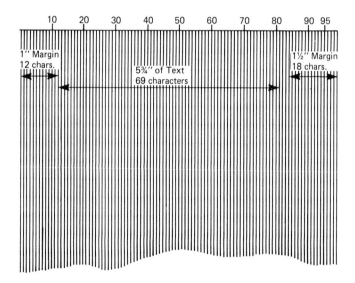

Figure 12

Should you use a ten-pitch printer, you will have only eighty-two spaces across the entire sheet. A one-inch margin on the left then would start printing on space 11, and the last space to be printed would be space 67. You would have a maximum of fifty-seven spaces in your line.

If you were using your printer at 15 CPI, the page would be 123 spaces across; to have a one-inch left margin and a one-and-a-half-inch right margin, your printing would start on space 16 and end on space 101, giving you an eighty-six printed line.

And if you are using proportional spacing, calculate the grid on an 11 CPI basis. Your margins would be set at 12 and 74, but it is difficult to know exactly how many characters would be in each line. It all depends on the words in your text: words with lots of "m"s and "w"s take up much more room than words with narrow letters, such as "it" and "if."

Most work is done using 12 CPI. Analyze the kinds of work you do most often. Set up some standard margin settings for each of the types of work. Print them on a 3″ × 5″ card or small piece of paper and tape it to the side of your monitor. Then whenever you want to set your system up to work on one of these typical jobs, you have your margin settings at your fingertips.

5
New Keys: wx o.

5.1 THIRD FINGER KEYS

In this chapter you are introduced to the last of the five vowels, the full stop ("."), and the "w" and "x." These are all third finger keys. Figure 13 shows where they are located.

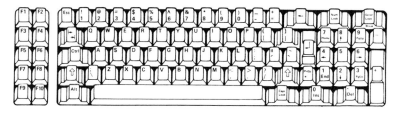

Figure 13

Try using your third fingers up and down at the slight angle you are now getting quite used to, so that you feel the distance and direction for these keys:

sw sw sw sw ws ws ws sw ws sx sx sx xs xs xs sx xs sx xs wx wxs sxw
swx sxw lo lo lo ol ol ol l. l. l. .l .l .o o. .o o. .lo ol. .lo ol. lo. lo. l.o l.o
wowowow x.x.x.x .so os. wlx xlw woslx. .xlsow .lowsx w.oxsl ls.xow

Again, you will probably find that using only the fingers of your right hand takes a bit more concentration, since you also have to use the right thumb to create spaces. (Just why the left thumb is not used is a mystery to us. We have never really been satisfied with any answer we've heard. Perhaps the person who created the QWERTY method had had an unfortunate accident and had use only of the right thumb. Anyway, when you think space, think right thumb.)

Your range of possible words has grown enormously with the addition of the "o" and "w" to your repertory. Here are some varieties of combinations to try:

word door weird woe waver waffle over our mouse voice ferric oxide
oxen exceed excel illume immemorial jealous jackal jackass jovial joker
kilometre cook Korea look cool loom loose looser loud louder

Keep typing these words over and over again until you can produce them on your screen with some degree of ease and without looking at your fingers and the keys while you do it. The point at the present is to increase the range of your fingers and the combinations of their use without any feeling of stress.

Here are some additional words to try (note how you can keep building words up):

xenon Xerox Xmas oxide oxford Oxford oxpecker express exorcise exile
exercise exclude excuse exam Max exclaim ax axe axes axiom axis axle
well weaver wax waxworks walk walker wad daw jackdaw waif wail wake
wakeful wade William willow Wilson wild widow wicker wick wreck
wrecker worm world worldwide work workweek work force word
wordless word order oar oak oasis clock odd odder ode odium odour
odourless odorous of if for from off offer office officer oil oil slick oiler
oil well o.k. okra old older olden olive oral oracle ore Osaka ourself
ourselves over overdose overcome overdue overdo overall overview
override overrode overwork

With the range of letters you can now use, try some short (rather banal) sentences:

William wakes for a walk.
William walks off.
William closed a door of a room.

5.2 SPACING RULES

As a general rule, you press the space bar once between words and after a comma (",") and a semicolon (";"). You press the space bar twice after a full stop ("."), a colon (":"), a question mark ("?"), and an exclamation mark ("!"). Thinking about that extra press after the stronger punctuation marks takes a bit of getting used to, but it soon will seem very natural.

Try some full stops with two spaces, just to get the feel of the movement:

. . . .

and some more sentences:

I like Osaka, a cool place in Asia.
I also like Miami, for me a real cool place.
Xmas in Oxford is wild.
Officer Wilson works worldwide.
Once Miami was dark.
Olive oil smells weird.
Sam exclaimed over Osaka.

5.3 FUNCTIONS

Set your margins for a sixty-character line. That's a good length for a report or book, since it gives you margins on both sides for corrections and revisions. For an 8½″ × 11″ page using a twelve-pitch printer, you have forty-two spaces of margin. Put twenty-one spaces on either side if you want the text to be centred on the page.

Word Wrap

Start typing some of your words from Chapters 4 and 5. Note the fact that when you come to the end of a line, any word you have not as yet finished drops down automatically to the next line where you finish typing it. (Note: this feature is provided in most but not all word-processing programs.) If you just finish a word at the end of the line, the cursor automatically drops down to the beginning of the next line, where you begin typing the next word. This feature on computers is called "word wrap." With this feature, you *never* use your return key to end a normal line of typing. You just keep typing and the system ends each line for you as you fill the sixty spaces up, or nearly up. (If you go back to the beginning and change your line length to forty spaces, the system will automatically rewrap the words as you move your cursor down through the document line by line.) In typing, your return key is used only at the end of a paragraph or to give you extra lines of space between blocks of copy (but it may be used to perform other computer functions when executing commands).

Subheadings

If you have a long document—a report or a book—you can have the system start and end each page at a certain place on each sheet of paper. Once you put in those instructions, the system will apply them automatically through the entire document. However, you may use short subtitles (generally called "subheadings" or "heads") from time to time throughout the document to break up the text into more manageable pieces and to give your readers some idea of what they are going to find in that section. Sometimes your subheadings will fall on the bottom line of the paper. It's an awkward and confusing location; so you may want to end your page two or three lines sooner than normal, and your subheading then will be at the top of the next page. Your software manual describes a series of steps to follow to end a page early. With IBM PC/EasyWriter program, as an example, you enter the insert mode at the beginning of the line following the last one you want printed, type in the word ".EJECT" (the full stop in front of the word alerts the system to the fact that this is a command, since spaces always follow full stops in regular text), press the return key, and exit from the insert mode. Whatever your program, there is a similar method of ending a page a line or two shorter than your regular page margin settings. This command instructs the printer to stop printing at the location it "reads" the command, to advance the sheet of paper through the printer, and to start printing the next page according to the normal margin settings.

5.4 JUSTIFICATION OR RAGGED RIGHT

There are two ways of treating your right-hand margin: You can leave it "ragged" or you can "justify" it. Only very seldom do all the letters of a line end up at the last space of the line. Sometimes you see it work out just right and your typed line ends exactly on the right-hand margin. More often you start typing what seems to be the last word of the line, but it goes over the margin by one or more characters, and then the entire word drops down to the beginning of the line below. Because this happens at different space locations down through the page, the right-hand margin is quite uneven. This is called "ragged right." Typewriters normally produce ragged right margins; and many magazines and some books increasingly are designed to have ragged right margins. If you are preparing a report or the manuscript of a book, ragged right margins are very acceptable. To achieve a ragged right margin, you do nothing. Just print out your document as the word wrap falls.

Many word-processing programs, however, have a feature that justifies your printout. You may not notice this feature on the characters on the screen. They may look just the same as they always do—with ragged right margins. But the printer will either add tiny amounts of space between words across the line or squeeze the words closer together, so that the right-hand margin is straight up and down just like the left-hand margin. You need to find the "justification" commands in your software manual. They are often a part of the printing menu, since they are instructions to the printer about how the copy is to be printed.

The usual procedure for justifying is to call up the proper menu and enter the "justify" command (with the IBM EasyWriter program for instance, you merely press the "J" key and then the return key). You will then probably need to realign your document, that is, to instruct the system to reorganize your line ending locations. This is necessary because the lines might be too tight or too loose to justify properly. Your system goes through the arithmetical calculations for each line and occasionally moves a word up or down a line. When the aligning function is finished (and it may take some time), you can then send the document to the printer for printing. Some lines may have too much space between the words; to correct the appearance of these lines you will need to hyphenate. (Chapter 7 deals with that function.)

6
New Keys: tg yh

6.1 MORE FIRST FINGER KEYS

So far you have worked the first, second, and third fingers up and down one row from the home position. Now we add another line of keys for the first finger. In this chapter we concentrate on two of the movements (across and up), and in the next chapter we will focus on the third movement (across and down). Figure 14 shows the position of the left-hand first finger for "g" and "t" and of the right-hand first finger for "h" and "y."

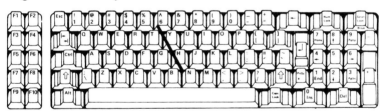

Figure 14

The first fingers are the only ones that cover two slanting vertical lines of keys. They each cover the vertical keys above and below their home positions. They also move in toward the centre of the keyboard one vertical line from home and cover those keys as well. Try some simple movements at first to get used to the direction and location of these keys.

Left-hand Fingers

For the first finger of the left hand:

fgfgfgfgfgfgfg fgf gfg gfg fgf fgf ggf ffg fg gf gfgfgf fgfgfg

(Be sure to bring the first finger back over the home key whenever you press "g.") Now go up and to the left:

ft ft ft ft tf tf tf ft ftttf tffft ftf tft ftf

And now mix the four keys on the home line and the line above for the first finger of the left hand:

frtg gtrf fr rt tr gr rg gr tr gr tr gr fr

Try some words:

tame frame rail frail trail grail rave grave trave grove trove rove roil toil foil

Now work on the four keys for the first finger (home and up) of the right hand:

jh jh jh jh hj hj hj jhhj jhhj jhj hjh jy jy jy yj yj yj yj jyyj yjjy jyj yjy.

And mix them up a bit:

jhyu uyhj juyh jhyu yuhj jhyu jujyjh

There are some basic combinations you can begin to put together that will come up continually in your typing:

th th th th the the the the there there there their their they they them them

The "th" combination is heavily used in English. Slightly less used is the "wh" combination:

where where why why why whether whether wheel wheel whim whim what what wharf wharf wheat wheat who who whole whole wholesome white white white

Another often used combination is "ght":

eight eight ought ought right might light fight fought fought fright tight sight

In many words, the "t" is not used:

rough tough dough slough

Still another combination is "ly," which makes an adverb from adjectives:

just justly most mostly high highly low lowly last lastly third thirdly fifth fifthly free freely faithful faithfully effectual effectually rough roughly

Yet another combination you often encounter is "ch":

church children child crutch chemistry chess chessmen choke clock inch niche charm charge chattel charter character characteristic

You can now type some rather more meaningful sentences:

You are charmed right out of your head. Yes, I surely am. I had little idea that I could use the keys so well. Tomorrow is the first day of the rest of my life. It is good to eat a full meal to start the day. We left the house soon after the stars came out. The lake was calm, the sky clear, the yacht steady. The oil slick moved out slowly across the water.

Remember, each time you sit in front of your screen, spend a few extra minutes typing words from the keys you already know. By now, you are probably finding that the keys you learned at first come much easier to you. Now that you have more keys at your disposal, there is more interest in getting combinations and words to flow out from your fingers. Don't be concerned so much about speed as about developing a steady, effortless rhythm. "Slow and steady" is more productive in typing than spurts of stops and starts.

Also, keep practising on your imaginary keyboard when you are away from the computer.

6.2 FUNCTIONS

Centre Text

One of the nice functions that the computer will automatically perform for you when you are typing is to centre your text between your margins. (It may also centre text over columns, but most often the centring feature is used in reports to centre titles.) Normally, this feature is performed by putting the cursor where you want the line to centre (usually halfway between the left and right margins). Then you call up the appropriate menu (see your software manual) and press the key for centring ("C" in the IBM PC/EasyWriter program). As you type the line, it will build out on either side from the cursor location. When you have finished the line, press the return key. Your cursor drops down to the next line and you are back in the regular typing mode. Find the centring function in your software manual and play with it until you can use it with ease. Then try to put this memo on your system:

MEMO

16 March 1989

From:–Tom Smith
To:–Jim Dresser

Re:–Costs

Our study of costs for the toys this Christmas shows that we must raise the whole value structure of what we receive from our customers. Effective tomorrow, make those sales tags give us higher rewards for our efforts.

(If the language seems somewhat stilted, it's because we're waiting for "n" and "p.")

Copies

Sometimes you want to copy your document for file and reference purposes. There are two ways to do this. The first is to make a copy of your document on a copy disk or backup disk. Because disk errors can inexplicably be introduced into document disks, it is wise to keep a backup of any document you think is important. Many kinds of software programs and the hardware supporting then usually enable you to make a copy of your entire document disk. In the more powerful systems, you can make a copy of a particular document from your working disk to a backup disk. By using this more limited copying of important documents instead of entire disks, you don't have to copy all the files on a working disk that you have no interest in keeping.

Your software manual will lead you through the copying process step-by-step. Be sure that you follow the steps just as you are directed. Pay special attention to any prompts that appear on your screen and tell you which disk to put into which drive. There is nothing more aggravating than copying an empty disk onto your master document (you got the wrong disk in the wrong drive and ended up losing what you really wanted two copies of)!

Also, each time you go back over the document on your working disk to upgrade and revise it, recopy the revised version over the old backup copy. By doing this, you won't inadvertently use the older version, which is now out-of-date and incorrect.

Hard Copy Duplicates

You may also wish to have a hard copy printout of your document for file purposes or for editing with a pencil or pen. If you know you will want such a copy when you first print it out, simply tell your system then that you want two copies instead of one. Your software manual has the instructions. This entry is usually one that has to be made in the print menu each time you call out that menu for printing purposes. Usually the menu asks you for the number of copies you want; you enter the number and press the return key. The system will print through the entire document in sequence from beginning to end for the number of times you ordered.

Automatic Page Numbering

If you are printing a document with more than one page—any length from a 2-page letter to a 600-page novel—you may wish to have the system automatically number your pages as you print them out. Here again, you have to refer to your software manual for instructions. You will be told that you can number from page 1 or leave it blank and start numbering from page 2. For reports you may want to number from page 1; for letters, from page 2. Perhaps your document is Chapter 7 of The Great British Novel; if so, you would want to pick up the numbering from the last page of Chapter 6—and so you instruct the system when you give it numbering instructions.

You can also place the numbers at appropriate locations on the sheet of paper. You might want them centred at the top or bottom of the sheet of paper:

23

Or you might want a hyphen on either side:

-23-

Or you might want them at the top outside margin if you are going to photocopy your report on both sides of the copy paper. The even numbers are left-hand pages:

14

And the odd numbers are right-hand pages:

15

So pages 14 and 15 face each other in your report and the page numbers are at the top (or bottom) on the outside margins—easy to find when leafing through the report. Your software program will tell you how to place the numbers at the desired location on the page and (on some programs only) how to alternate them automatically from one side to the other as the printing runs out.

Print from Screen

It may be that you have a very short memo that you want to print. If you have the margins you want already set into the system, in many systems you don't have to go into the print menu in order to print out that memo. You simply follow the instructions on how to "print from screen." This will result in the copy (less any commands) that you see on the screen being printed out just as you see it. This is an excellent way of sending short messages. If you want a copy for yourself, just repeat the print-from-screen command (remembering to scroll back to the right page before printing it a second time from the screen).

Print Part of a Document

It is also possible to instruct your system to print only a part of a document. This is most useful when you have found some errors, for example, on page 34. You've gone into the document and made the corrections, but you don't want an extra copy of pages 1–33 (nor do you want to spend the time and paper they take to print out). You tell the system to print "from 34" and print "to 34." By doing that, only page 34 is printed. If you have made so many changes on page 34 that it throws the rest of the report out of sequence, then you can tell the system to print "from 34" and it will start with page 34 and go on through to the end of the document.

Stop Printing

Sometimes you may be printing a long document and you want to stop the printing. You notice something you want to change or you are called away and don't want to leave it printing out while you are gone. Your software manual will give you the steps to stop printing. You may even have two choices here: one is to stop temporarily until you signal the system to recommence printing where it left off; the other is to stop and cancel the print order.

Paper Feeders

Many personal and home computers use a dot matrix printer with a tractor feeder. The tractor feeder has tiny ratchets (wheels with spokes) that mesh into holes in continuous form paper and pull the paper through the feeder line by line as the printer is printing. When the document is finished printing, you then have to separate the pages and tear them apart along the perforated lines that mark out the pages of continuous form paper. You also have to tear off the side edges that have the holes. Some printers are able to take single sheets of paper. These have to be hand-fed, unless you have added an automatic single-sheet feeder. Some people have a letterhead printed on continuous form paper and use it as part of their regular business or personal correspondence. Others use letterhead sheets (business or personal) in a printer that can handle single sheets. When you set up your printing instructions, instruct your printer which method of sheet feeding you are using. You will find those directions in your software manual, if your system has these options.

7
New Keys: b n - ' "

7.1 MORE FIRST FINGER KEYS

In Chapter 6 we used the first fingers across and up; now we move them down.

Left-hand Finger

With the left first finger, press the "f" and "b" keys:

fbfbfb bfbfbf fb bf fb bf

And all the left first finger keys:

frtgbvf fvbgtrf fr frt trf fgt
fgr fgb fbg fvb bvf fbv fgf

Start from different keys:

tgf trf tgb tvb tbv tgv trb brf
bvf bgt brg brt gvb grt gbv gft
grb brv gvt brt bvt bfr btf bgf
brv vbr vgb vft vtr vrg

Do these kinds of patterns without looking at the keyboard, and by thinking which letters you want to strike. It will take some time to match which of the six first finger positions go with which letter.

Right-hand Finger

Do the same with the right first finger, adding the "n" key to your collection:

jnjnjn njnjnjnj jn nj jn nj

And mix them up:

jnh jhn jun jyn jmn jhm jny jum jyh unh unm umn uyh yjh yhn yjm yhm
muh mny mhu mnj myj mnj hmu hjn hyn hym hymn myh mnu mhn
mhm mjy mun nju

Between the two first fingers, you control twelve keys. The "j" and the "v" are the least used of the twelve.

Later in this chapter, we will add some important punctuation marks as shown in Figure 15. But for now, we want to go further into the use of the "n" and "b" keys.

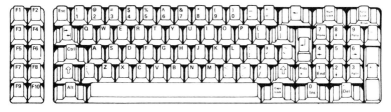

Figure 15

Here are some important combinations that occur in many words:

  ing: living loving riding siding climbing riming dining wining winning aiming losing loosening getting growing craving raving dividing subtracting adding trying saving starving striving
  ment: tenement establishment document government lineament judgment monument
  tion: ration nation determination radiation levitation osculation imitation initiation irritation triangulation sedation
  sion: mission commission remission vision lesion revision
  be: because bewilder bemuse betides between better best belt benevolent bench beast beach bed beef

  Try some "nth" combinations:

ninth tenth eleventh nth degree

And some sentences:

Now is the time for all good men to come to the aid of their country.
America is the land of the free and the home of the brave.
My business is making fifteen times more than it made five years ago.
I have visited each of the United States, including Alaska and Hawaii.
Johnny was serving in the Navy in the days when they had navy beans
for lunch.
The wind blew to gale force, causing the large tree in the back garden
to fall on the garage.

Watch the Screen, Not the Keys

Keep working on these sentences, and ones like them that you make
up, until you feel increasingly comfortable watching only your
screen—not the keys, even though your fingers pause over the keys
every once in a while as you figure out which key to press. It is our
assumption that you will be creating most of your copy directly on
your screen, rather than copying material from a manuscript that is
located alongside your keyboard. If we were teaching you to type for a
living, we would say "keep your eyes on the copy at the side of your
typewriter—not even on the paper in the machine." But we don't
believe most personal computer users will use the keyboard like a
professional typist uses a typewriter. So, think the words, match the
fingers to the thoughts, and watch the results appear on the screen.

A Business Letter

Now is the time to try a short business letter. The standard form these
days is to use as few keystrokes as necessary, since keystrokes are time
(and the possibility of errors that take time to correct), and time is
money. Therefore, business letters are usually entirely blocked to the
left margin, with no indentations throughout the letter. Paragraphs
are separated by a line of space. There is no punctuation after the
elements of the address. So pretend you've had an enjoyable flight
with extra care being given to you by your flight crew and you want to
say something nice about them:

December 23, 1988

Mr. John Airlines, Chairman
Crosscountry Airways 123 Flight Street
London, W1

Dear Mr. Airlines:

Recently I flew on Crosscountry Flight 123 from Birmingham to London. An urgent business matter had arisen on very short notice. I did not have time to make normal travel arrangements.

At every encounter with your airline's staff, I met with understanding, and even more vital, with the assistance needed to get me on my way with the minimum of trouble and inconvenience. From reservations to flight crew and attendants to ground services at Birmingham, Crosscountry came through with style to get me to London on time and in a winning frame of mind. I concluded the matter there successfully during the day and got back to Birmingham early in the evening.

My thanks to the crew of Flight 123 on December 15 and to all your ground staff.

Sincerely yours,

Robert T. Traveller

7.2 SOME PUNCTUATION KEYS

There are a couple of important punctuation keys that are outside the normal range of the immediate home pattern. The first is the hyphen and the underline key. It is up on the top row to the right.

When the key is pressed (with the right little finger) in the regular mode, a hyphen ("-") is produced.

When the key is pressed in the shift mode (use the left little finger to press the shift key), an underline ("_") is produced.

Of all the keys on the top row, this is one that you should work at being able to reach without looking at the key.

Hyphens

Hyphens are used to create compound words:

> well-done
> well-mannered
> well-established
> decision-making
> time-consuming
> second-hand
> self-reliant
> high-level
> all-inclusive
> brother-in-law

Hyphens are also used in dividing a word at a syllable break at the end of a line, so that part of the word drops down to the line below. Some computer software programs for word processing use have a hyphenation section in the program. (The IBM PC/EasyWriter program, which we have been using as an example, does not have such a hyphenation feature.) Where there is a hyphenation program, there are usually three kinds of hyphens that can be produced. The first is a "hard hyphen," one in which you merely press the hyphen key. This produces a firm character in the system that acts just like any other letter key you might press. Since the computer understands a "word" to be any group of characters between two spaces, the compound word "all-inclusive" is considered by the computer to be a single word. If any character in "all-inclusive" goes over the right margin, the entire "word" "all-inclusive" will drop to the line below. This can make a big hole in a line if the "word" is as long as "non-English-speaking." The computer whose software has a hyphenation program solves this by giving you a "soft hyphen" option. By pressing a control key at the same time as you press the hyphen key, you can make the "word" that has a hyphen in it break just after the hyphen if the end of the word happens to fall outside the right margin. If you rearrange the text by adjusting the margins or adding/deleting copy, causing the hyphenated word to appear in the middle of a line, the computer will join them together properly.

As a working rule, you should use the hard hyphen for telephone numbers (555-1234), which should never be broken between two lines. You might also use it for compound words in the middle of a line when you know you are not going to revise the copy or its format. Otherwise, use the soft hyphen for compound words.

The third kind of hyphen in a system that uses a hyphenation program is an automatic word hyphenation option that serves as a syllable breaker for words you want to divide at the end of a line. This is sometimes especially useful if you are justifying the right margin and want part of a word left on a line, so that the space between words won't be so large when the line is spread out to fill both margins. The system normally will stop at the last word in a line that extends over the margin. It will ask you whether you want to break (hyphenate) the word, and if so, where. You move your cursor to the character that is the first one you want to go down to the line below and execute the hyphenation command. A hyphen will appear on the screen just where the cursor was, and the rest of the word will drop to start the next line. If, later on, you rearrange the copy by adjusting the margins or adding/deleting words and the hyphenated word then falls in the middle of a line, the computer will join the word together without the "syllable division" hyphen having any effect when the word is printed out. Normally the syllable division hyphen will be suppressed on the screen when the parts of the word have been joined due to text rearrangement.

If your program does not have a hyphenation capability, you can manually "fool" the system into giving you a hyphen at the end of a line when you want one. If you want to divide a word that goes over the right margin, simply enter the hyphen at the appropriate syllable, then press your space bar a couple of times, and continue with the rest of the word; thus you get "hypno- sis." The system reads "hypno-" as a single word since it is a stream of characters between spaces; "sis" is a second unique word to the computer and therefore it will drop the entire word "sis" to the next line if the final "s" or "is" goes over the margin. You could also divide the word as "hyp- nosis" and the "nosis" would drop. You can do the same with compound words that fall at the end of a line and extend over, such as "self- reliant."

You will face an editing problem, however, if you rearrange the copy and the system joins these two "words" on the same line. Since the hyphen and the two spaces are each "hard" characters, they do not disappear when the words are joined. You will need then to delete the hyphen and the spaces in order to actually join the word together properly.

The hyphen is also used to serve as a dash. The usual method of typing the dash is to use two hyphens, connecting the words separated by the dash with no spaces:

One long winter--I think it was back in 1888-- the Thames froze so thick that horse-drawn carriages used the river instead of the bridge.

Underline

To underline words on a computer, it is necessary to read your software manual on underlining. You will need to define the area within which underlining is to take place by pressing format or control keys at both ends of the section to be underlined. You may or may not actually use the "_" key, depending on the software program. When your printer prints out the underlined copy, you will note that it prints out the underline first and then goes back and prints out the complete line (or it may do the reverse, print out the line and then go back and print only the underlining).

If, however, you want to type in a line instead of a name, you use the underline key:

During Prime Minister _____'s administration, the budget was balanced.

A letter quality printer (one that uses a printwheel) will join underline characters to make a single line; dot matrix printer underline characters will usually have a tiny space between each one.

Quotation Marks

The other punctuation key that is introduced in this chapter is also a right little finger key. It is between the home position and the return key. Pressed in the regular mode, it is ('); and pressed in the shift mode ("). It is most generally used for indicating quotations in speech. In standard English, the double quotation mark (") is "junior" to the single quotation mark ('). Thus, a quote uses single quotation marks and a quote within a quote uses double quotation marks:

She said, 'How many times have I heard him say, "Don't put off until tomorrow what you can do today."'

In American English, the order of quotation mark seniority is reversed.

The marks are also used for the following:

the apostrophe ('):

don't I'll Mary's

foot (') and inch ("):

He is 6′3″ tall. Here's an 8¼″ × 11¾″ sheet of paper.

minute (') and second ("):

The ship's latitude is 40° 10′6″ N and 73°4′3″ W.

Double quotation marks are also used for singling out a word:

The word "arroyo" is a Spanish word to denote a dry gulch that may
have flash floods from rains in mountains far removed from the gulch
itself, so a wall of water can rush down an arroyo on a clear, sunny day.
This word has been taken into American English usage. The Arabic work
"wadi" denotes the same kind of gulch, and the English have adopted that
word instead of "arroyo." Perhaps that's because the English were active
for centuries in the Middle East, whereas the Spanish were the first
European settlers in the American Southwest.

7.3 FUNCTIONS

Search

An extremely useful program that nearly all computers have is the
ability to search for a particular character or stream of characters. The
cursor will stop every time that character or stream of characters
occurs in your document. You may use this function to go through a
long document to find a particular word or phrase.

Search and Replace

Even more useful is the ability to replace that character or stream of
characters with others. Your computer can do this on a prompted
basis—the cursor stops at each occurrence of the search word or
phrase and you are asked whether you want to replace it with your
replace word or phrase and then continue the search, or whether you
want to continue on to the next occurrence of the search word or
phrase without replacing it at this point.
    Following the instructions in your software manual, you call up the

search and replace menu from one of your menu listings. Following the prompts on your screen, you enter the word or phrase you want the system to search for; then you enter the word or phrase you want to replace the search word or phrase; then you tell the system whether you want this done automatically at every instance or whether you want to be able to make the decision about replacement at each instance. All you have to do is execute the search and replace command, and let the computer do your work for you.

If, for instance, you are typing a long report that uses the term "ferromagnetic" often, and you want to save time, you might choose a symbol that you know will not appear in the document and type that symbol instead of the word "ferromagnetic." For example, you might use the "@" symbol. When you have finished writing your report, run a global (through the entire document) search and replace sequence to replace automatically every instance of "@" with the stream of characters "ferromagnetic." Because "ferromagnetic" will occur at different locations in the sentence, use the appropriate punctuation with the "@" symbol:

whereas some substances are @, other are not
The test is whether the substance is @.
a @ alloy is required
then it cannot be called @.

If you don't want to use a symbol, use an abbreviation of the word in a combination of letters that do not normally occur in English words. For "ferromagnetic" you might use "fmg," since that combination is rarely found in words. If you used "fer," the program would stop at the "fer" part of "interfere." The longer your search stream of characters, the less chance there is for the search to stop on other words than the specific word or phrase you are searching for.

If you wanted identical letters, for instance, to go to "Mr. Robinson" and "Mrs. Adams," you could type the first letter to Mr. Robinson. Then for the second letter, do a search and replace with "Mrs. Adams" for "Mr. Robinson."

If in your report you sometimes misspelled "ferromagnetic" as "feromagnetic," a search and replace sequence ("ferromagnetic" replacing "feromagnetic") would leave all the properly spelled instances untouched but would correct all your spelling errors.

Sometimes some words are to be capitalized and others are not. For instance, in writing an article about Trafalgar Square, you may somewhere want to comment on the appearance of the square. As you are writing the article, you know you are occasionally confusing the use of "Square"—a proper name of this particular square—and "square"—a reference to squares in general, of which Trafalgar Square is a specific instance. When you've finished the article, you want to check on whether you really want the word with or without a capital "S." So, run a search and replace program—"square" for "Square"—on a prompted basis, and make up your mind each time you see "square" whether you want it capitalized. Then run the program the other way—"Square" for "square"—and decide this time whether you want the word in lowercase letters.

One way of avoiding stopping at every instance of a combination of common letters that make up a short word is to include the spaces before and after the word as part of the search and replace elements. For instance, if you often type "fo" for "of" and you want to avoid stopping at every word that contains an "fo" element somewhere in it, search for "(space) fo (space)" and replace it with "(space) of (space)."

8
New Keys: qz p / ?

8.1 MORE LITTLE FINGER KEYS

In this chapter we conclude the introduction to all the letters of the alphabet. The final keys are little finger keys. The left little finger keys up and down from home position are ones you will not use all that often, simply because English does not often use "q" and "z." The right little finger up from home position is used regularly, the "p." But the right little finger down is used so seldom that you'll probably have to look for it when you want it. The regular mode is a slash ("/"), and the shift mode is a question mark ("?").

Figure 16 shows how these keys appear on the keyboard. Try them for a while to get used to using your little fingers up and down and to feel their location and distance from home.

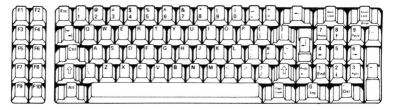

Figure 16

Try:

> qaz zaq qa aq qa zao qaz za az
> p;//;p p; ;p p; ;p//;
> p;//;p ;? ?; ?;p p;?

The question mark will slow you up somewhat because you have to remember to shift at the same time as press the "?" key.

In general English usage, "q" is always followed by a "u." The only exceptions are words of places and people that are transliterated from Arabic as well as some abbreviations. Try a variety of "q" words:

quaint quantity quality Quaker quake quail quill queen queenly quart
quarter question query Quebec quilt quit quite quote quotable quiz
quizzical quartz

Some Arabic names:

Qatar Qaddafi

Then some abbreviations:

qty.
Q.E.D. (use your caps-lock mode for this)
QM QB, qlty, qt. qtr.

There are few English words that begin with "z." Among them are:

zebra zero zeppelin zip zing zoology zoo zone zombie zinnia zeal zany zap

There are names of foreign places that start with "Z":

Zaire Zambesi Zagreb Zamboanga Zambia Zimbabwe Zion Zuyder Zee
(Tappan Zee)

And some names of people and peoples:

Zulu Zachary Zephaniah Zola Zeus Zanzibari Zapata New Zealanders
Flo Ziegfeld

And some words with "z" in the middle:

raze razzle dazzle freeze froze frozen freezing maze amaze amazing craze
crazy lazy lazily doze dozen

Many "pr," "ph," and "pl" combinations occur in English:

telephone pharmacy phantom phenomenon Philadelphia Philip
photograph telegraph graphology physician phrase mesomorph produce
product promise premise appropriate appropriately approximate price
appraise prevent prevention primary primarily print prince Prince Philip
prance prayer practice property protect protection project proof profound

appliance pliant plastic plaster complete planet plant plane play play-by-play plate platform plenty plentiful plea plead pled plight plough plow plot pluck plum plug plumber plunge plus plush ply

Now try some sentences that use the new keys:

If I go outside, will I freeze my toes?
I'd like to take the *Queen Elizabeth II* to
Zanzibar/Tanzania/Zimbabwe.
There are three quarts of antifreeze in the radiator.
How many do you want—a dozen?
No, three's plenty.
Please, may I have some frozen custard?
I'd like a whole quart of chocolate banana.
I think the white flowers by the roadside are Queen Anne's lace, and the red ones—over there near the oak tree—are devil's paintbrush.
My favourite California wine is zinfandel, especially with barbecued hamburgers. But it's also a wine that goes well with haute cuisine.
My zodiac sign is Aquarius; what's yours?
Is your birthstone an opal?
D day was 6/6/44, sometimes called "the longest day."

And a business letter:

December 17, 1989
Mr. John Emery, Chairman
MNO Products Ltd.
321 Corporation Road
Manchester M32 0XX

Dear Mr. Emery:

This is to express my dissatisfaction with your Whatsit. I recently purchased one from our local hardware store.

Not only did the Whatsit fail to perform according to your advertising claims, but it broke right in the middle of an important job. We lost the better part of a week repairing the damage done by the Whatsit when it broke. That used time that could have been productively spent in furthering our business.

I am returning the broken Whatsit to you and am requesting a full refund—including my shipping costs—by return mail.

Thank you for your prompt attention to this matter.

Sincerely,

Martin Perturbed
copy: Jamison, McCreedy and Lazarus

And a happier memo:

MEMORANDUM

June 1, 1990
From: R. S. Batts
To: All personnel

Subj: Holiday and company Annual Dinner

Normally the Annual Dinner is held on the 24th of August each year. However, this year the 24th falls on a Saturday with the following Monday (August 26) being a Bank Holiday, enabling people to enjoy a long weekend.

I know many of you are planning to take a weekend away with friends and family at that time. Rather than complicate plans with our company dinner on Saturday the 24th, I am rescheduling the Annual Dinner to Friday, September 6, to be held at the Charlton Hotel, Queen Street. Please plan to be at the Europa Suite no later than 8:00 p.m. when drinks and then dinner will be served.

The company is providing food and entertainment for all. Keaton's Jazz Quintet will be the band for the evening.

Sorry, spouses only; no friends this year.

Have a great Bank Holiday and see you on September the 6th!

8.2 FUNCTIONS

Tabs

Setting and controlling tabs is a key function in shaping a document that has columns or indentations. Your software manual gives you directions on how to enter the tab settings. Usually you need to go into a menu that gives you the option of choosing several functions, one of which is tab control. When you call up the tab menu, you enter the kinds of tabs you want at the grid locations on the ruler where you want them. With the IBM PC/ EasyWriter software, you can enter as many as fifteen tab stops; other software programs will have other maximum numbers of tabs.

A tab moves the cursor from where it is to the next tab stop on that line. For instance, you may be writing a book and wish to have each paragraph opening indented five spaces from the left margin. Rather than space over five spaces with your right thumb at the beginning of each paragraph, go into your tab menu and place a tab stop at the space number that is five spaces in from your left margin. If you've placed your left margin at "12," your paragraph indent tab stop will be placed at "17." Then, when you finish writing a paragraph, you press the return key. This ends the last line of the paragraph as it falls on the line and moves the cursor down to start the next line. You then press the "tab" key with your left little finger. Reach up and out with your finger just beyond the "Q" key. When you press the tab key, the cursor will jump to space 17—ready to begin your paragraph at proper indent.

In the computer, pressing that tab key creates one character, not five "space" characters. If you delete that character, your copy will jump back to the left margin.

The tab function is very useful if you are writing dialogue with lots of short sentences that begin as paragraphs ("t" is "tab"; "r" is "return"):

t   'Never,' she said.r
t   'Why not?'r
t   'Well, just because ...'r
t   'You have to tell me!'r
t   She looked out of the window for a long time, her eyes moving back and forth as though she were reading her own thoughts.r
t   'Well?'r
t   'O.K.' she snapped, 'I just don't like pizza, that's all!'r

In the illustration above, the underline function is used instead of italics in order to give emphasis.

You also use tab settings for columnar work. Here's a table that is part of a balance sheet in making a financial report ("s" is space):

*Assets*r
r
t	Cash on handt	ss5,321.78r
t	Accounts Receivablet	s14,593.32r
t	Stocks and bondst	s45,782.16r
t	Propertyr	
t	t Buildingst	175,000.00r
t	t Equipmentt	s83,258.74r
t	t Furnituret	ss8,582.93r

r
t	Totalt	332,538.93r

r
*Liabilities*r

r
t	Short-term loanst	ss5,158.79r
t	Long-term loanst	s25,000.00r
t	Mortgaget	115,852.63r
t	Equipment notest	s36,259.58r
t	Accounts Payablet	ss4,373.61r

r
t	t Subtotalt	186,644.61r

r
t	Net wortht	145,894.32lr

r
t	Total liabilities andr	
	net wortht	332,538.93r

In this illustration, three tab stops were placed in the document: The first was three spaces in from the left margin of the document; the second was four more spaces in from that; and the third was about two thirds over toward the right margin of the document. It is necessary to visualise how you want your final document to look—even to sketch it out on a blank sheet of paper—before you actually set all your tabs. When you set them and print out a page of your document, you may wish to adjust one or more of the tabs. If, for instance, in the illustration above, you decided you wanted the column of figures to be located three spaces farther over to the right, you merely go back into your tab menu at the point where you first entered it, delete the tab setting where it is at present, and enter a new tab setting three spaces farther to the right. Execute your tab menu and then (depending on the conventions of your program) run your cursor down the lines of your table. The computer will automatically move that last column over to the new tab setting as your cursor passes through the table.

In the illustration we just gave, "t" represents a press on the tab key; "r" is a press on the return key; and "s" is a press on the space bar. Your printed document will not show these nonprintable characters, of course; the result will look like this:

Assets

Cash on hand	5,321.78
Accounts Receivable	14,593.32
Stocks and bonds	45,782.16
Property	
Buildings	175,000.00
Equipment	83,258.74
Furniture	8,582.93
Total	332,538.93

Liabilities

Short-term loans	5,158.79
Long-term loans	25,000.00
Mortgage	115,852.63
Equipment notes	36,259.58
Accounts Payable	4,373.61
Subtotal	186,644.61
Net worth	145,894.32
Total liabilities and	
net worth	332,538.93

When using the tab on a computer, you need to understand the effect of entering a tab character. It will always push the word or phrase that follows over to the next tab stop position. For instance, if in our example you somehow had an extra tab character in a line, it would look like this:

t t t		Buildings
175,000.00		
Equipment		83,258.74

That extra tab character in front of "Buildings" pushed the word over to the next tab position. The "175,000.00" dropped down a line since there was no room left on the original line nor was there a tab stop in the line for the tab character immediately following "Buildings." That tab character took effect on the next line and pushed the number over to the next available tab stop location. In order to correct this problem, it is necessary to take out one of the three tab stops in front of "Buildings." "Buildings" will then jump back one tab stop location (which is where you want it). Depending on your system, "175,000" may jump back automatically to the tab stop location that "Buildings" had occupied (which also is where you want it), or you may have to delete a return character at the end of the "Buildings" line to bring the figure back up to that line. Once you get "Buildings" in the right location, you can always keep deleting the character immediately after "Buildings" until "175,000" is joined to the word: "Buildings 175,000." Then reenter your tab key with the cursor under the number "1" and the entire figure "175,000" will jump over to the proper tab stop location.

Move Tab Settings

You can move tab settings, usually, as a part of your block move functions, so when you move a table from one part of your document to another you take your tab settings as a part of that block. These settings are also saved when you file your document; and they are part of the document when you call it back to the screen for revision later on.

With a few systems (among them the IBM PC), you can move forward and backward to tab settings. You move forward by pressing the tab key; you move backward by pressing the tab key in the shift mode. Most systems move the tab only forward through the document.

Set up your margins with tab stop commands with the tab stops every seven spaces, and work on some five-letter words in columns:

cinch	pinch	lynch	finch	ditch	pitch	patch
night	fight	sight	light	might	tough	rough
joins	loins	leans	means	beans	teams	teems

Go back into your tab menu and set new tab stops every ten spaces, and work on some six-letter words in columns:

clinch	flight	plight	swatch	snitch	blight
slight	slough	enough	quench	wrench	trench
French	clench	blanch	trance	chance	France
choice	gleams	dreams	cleans	gleans	quakes

Flush Left Tab

Some more advanced word-processing software gives you an option of setting different kinds of tab commands. One is a "flush left tab." This is the kind of tab you have been using. The tab serves as a flush left margin and the word or phrase builds to the right of the tab stop location:

d̲reams   c̲leans

The underlined letter is where the flush left tab is located.

Flush Right Tab

Another is a "flush right tab." Here the tab stop serves as a flush right margin and the word or phrase builds to the left of the tab stop location:

Introduction

Here you want the word "introduction" to be at the far right of the text area, so you use the flush right tab to serve as the rightmost character and you type the word regularly; as you do so, it builds to the left instead of to the right of the tab stop.

Centre Tab

The third kind of tab is the "centre tab." Here the word builds character by character on either side of the tab stop. You may locate such a tab at the centre of the text line, if you want a centred heading or title:

CHAPTER 8

or you may place such a tab over the centre of a column for a column
heading:

River	Length	Continent
Nile	4,160	Africa
Amazon	4,080	South America
Yangtze	3,964	Asia
Mississippi-Missouri	3,740	North America
Ob-Irtysh	3,360	Asia
Huang He (Yellow River)	3,010	Asia
Zaire	2,880	Africa
Paraná	2,796	South America

This table has two flush left tab stop settings (for the length and
continent columns; the document margin serves as the flush left
margin for the river column). It has three centre tab stops above each
of those columns. The columns were entered first with the flush left tab
stop settings. Once the length of the various entries was clear, a new
tab setting was entered above the table with the centre tab stops. You
have to be sure, however, to return to your original flush left tab stop
settings after your one line of centred column settings in order to keep
the system from continuing to use those centre tab settings. You are, in
effect, changing your format by changing your tab settings. Note
where you consciously must make decisions to change your format:

The lengths of the principal rivers of the world are:r r

tm ct		ct	ct
t Rivert		Lengtht	Continentr
tm			
r			
Nile		flt 4,160	flt Africa

Note the format changes in your document due to the placement of
tabs. The tab commands are, of course, suppressed in the printout.
They give structure to the characters that are printed. The "tm" is
where you have introduced a "tab menu" sequence in order to set your
various kinds of tab stop settings. The "ct" are centre tab settings; and
the "flt" are flush left tab settings. If your system does not have the
centre tab capability, you would have to space over on that line to the
place where you wanted "River" and enter the word; then space over to
where you wanted "Length" and enter it; and the same with
"Continent."

Extract

The flush left tab setting is also useful for typing an extract. An extract is an extended quotation in the body of regular text. Rather than putting quotation marks around a lengthy quotation the usual practice is to separate the quotation from the regular copy by a line space and to indent the entire quotation. In some books it is indented on both the right and left margins, but we do not recommend this for general use in computer typing; indenting the left margin is sufficient. Try typing an example:

One of the most well-known books ever written about a river is entitled The Nile. It was written in German in 1935 by Emil Ludwig and has been translated into dozens of languages. It has the power to evoke dramatic and memorable images.

> The men stand like the birds. Through the ages they have adapted themselves to their surroundings like these birds of the swamp, with their gaunt limbs, thin necks, small heads, and stiltlike legs, which they use in turn, standing for hours in the swamp with one foot supported on the knee of the other leg; stalk men, crane men, lonely in the Nile lagoons.

Once having read such a book, one always looks for the realities that underlie the images. When sailing in the Nile's waters, a person who has read Ludwig's book will always look for crane men. He will even imagine that a man seen in the distance takes a cranelike pose, so that his senses may confirm what his imagination demands to see.

The entire extract—the quotation from Ludwig—was indented one tab stop at the beginning of each line. For a short extract like this, tabbing is easier than resetting the margins before and after the extract.

9
New Keys: 12345 !@#£%

9.1 NUMBERS AND SYMBOLS

All of the letters of the alphabet, several of the main functional keys (space bar, return, shift, backspace, caps lock, tab), and a couple of punctuation keys (- and ' ") have been introduced in this book with the strong insistence that you learn to use them without looking at the keys. Now we come to the number/ symbol row of keys on the top of your regular keyboard. (We *know* we're going to get into real trouble with typing purists for this next recommendation.) We suggest you familiarize yourself thoroughly with the location of these number / symbol keys so you can use them with ease, *but* we don't suggest you go through the agony of learning to type them without looking at them.

There are several sound reasons for this recommendation. One is that we are not preparing you to be a professional typist or to pass typing speed/accuracy tests in order to interview for a job; we want to make typing on your computer interesting and easy. A second reason is that you don't use numbers and symbols as often as you use the alphabet; trying to remember which finger to stretch up and out for the "!" symbol takes far longer and is less accurate than just looking—especially when you know the general location of what you are looking for. And a third reason is that if you use numbers constantly for entering data (sales, inventory, cash-flow projections, and the like), you'll use the ten-number pad for that entry, if you have one, or you'll get so used to the numbers on the top row that you will develop your own "top-row easy entry method." (When you are typing straight numbers, you might try positioning all your fingers on the top row, thereby creating a new "home row" for numbers.)

So, in this chapter and the next, we will introduce you to the numbers, show you which fingers normally go with which keys, and launch you with some examples. In doing so, we will strengthen the skills you have already learned.

This chapter covers the "left-hand numbers," that is, the numbers that are normally pressed by the left-hand fingers. Figure 17 shows these keys. Just move your left hand up at a slight angle so that your little finger passes the "Q" key on the way to "1." Your four fingers fall naturally: little finger on "1"; third finger on "2"; second finger on "3"; and first finger on "4." The first finger also moves to the right for the "5" key.

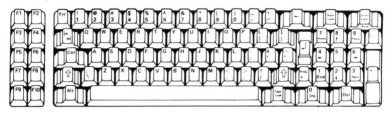

Figure 17

A note regarding number "1": Some people accustomed to using an early portable typewriter use the lowercase letter "l" for both "l" as in "lady" and "1" as in "1935." Then typewriters came into general use with a number "1" key, but these people found it easier to continue doing what they had become used to. If you picked up that habit, break it now. On your computer the two are very different electronic characters, however much their printout form may look similar. If you run any math programs, your computer just will not compute an "ell" character as a substitute for a "one" character. In passing, the same point can be made regarding the "zero" character and the capital "oh" character. Use the number keys for your numbers and the letter keys for your alphabet.

Try some combinations:

12345 54321 12345 54321 151141131121111 212 222 232 242 252 323 313
333 343 353 434 424 414 444 454 555 535 525 515

Now try reaching from the home position and combining numbers and words:

2 men 5 birds 3 cats 1 light 4 glasses 1 cup
3 saucers 5 spoons 2 plates
11 o'clock in the morning

Is Puerto Rico going to be the 51st state of America?
Canada is located at 42 degrees latitude.
He lives in Ascot and London WC2.
Is the drinking age in your country 21 or lower?
The Sears Tower in Chicago is taller than New York's World Trade
Centre, rising as it does to 1,454 feet.

Viscount Palmerstone became the British Prime Minister twice; he was
both the 22nd and the 24th premier of the country. The thermometer
hovered around the 14-degree mark, but with the windchill factor, it
seemed to be more like −35 degrees. To change inches to centimetres,
multiply the number of inches by a factor of 2.54; the result will be the
same distance expressed in centimetres.

The highest point in Ireland is the top of Carrantuohill; it is 3,415 feet
above sea level. And the republic has a population of 3,443,445.

Now for the symbols. On your computer it is necessary for you
actually to use the shift mode to produce the symbols. If you use the
cap-lock function, you will get capital letters for the alphabet, but you
will continue to get numbers for the number keys. The caps lock is not
an overall shift lock. So, whether you are typing caps and lowercase or
all caps, you still use the shift in conjunction with the symbol key to
enter a symbol.

The symbol for the number keys in the shift mode are:

$$! @ \# £ \%$$

You will use these different keys depending on the nature of your
work and interests. You will use the "!" if you write novels and articles,
or if you write personal letters with your computer. If you list
inventories or write invoices, you may use the "@" with some
regularity. The "#" is falling into general disuse; on many keyboards it
has been replaced by the "£" sign. Many of us are interested in and use
the "$" symbol at some time or other. And the "%" comes into
scientific and statistical writing. In other words, learn where the
symbols are that you are most likely to use in your typing; use the
appropriate finger to reach that key; and look for the rest when—and
if—you need them.

Try some typing samples that will build your flexibility to move
around the keyboard and perhaps be of some interest:

Winchester is situated 12 miles from Southampton at a point in the

Itchen Valley where the Downs converge from either side. It owes much
of its charm to its compactness. From the City Centre it is only 15
minutes' walk into open country by the river.

One can walk to the site of an Iron Age Settlement on St Catherine's
Hill; or on ecan follow a footpath along the river to St Cross
Hospital—surely the finest mediaeval almshouse in England. With its
Gatehouse, XIIth century church and quadrangle, in which the Brothers
live, St Cross gives an idea of what the monasteries of mediaeval England
must have looked like.

Of the royal castle all that remains is the Great Hall (XIIIth century).
The Hall was the meeting place of the first English Parliaments and was
the scene of several famous trials, notably that of Sir Walter Ralegh, who
was sentenced to death here. In the Castle Hall hangs the famous
Arthurian Round Table, the origin of which is unknown.

Just outside the City Wall is the College, founded in 1382, which has
ever since been one of England's leading schools. The mediaeval buildings
remain, and there have been some noteworthy later additions.

However, the glory of Winchester today is undoubtedly the Cathedral
with its vast nave, Norman transepts, magnificent altar screen and the
beautiful Close which surrounds it.

Now for an entirely different kind of format—a poem by the
English poet, John Donne, entitled *Song*:

Song

Go and catch a falling star,
   Get with child a mandrake root,
Tell me where all past years are,
   Or who cleft the Devil's foot;
Teach me to hear mermaids singing,
Or to keep off envy's stinging,
      And find
      What wind
Serves to advance an honest mind.

If thou b'st born to strange sights,
   Things invisible to see,
Ride ten thousand days and nights
   Till Age snow white hairs on thee;
Thou, when thou return'st, wilt tell me
All strange wonders that befell thee,
      And swear
      Nowhere
Lives a woman true, and fair.

If thou find'st one, let me know,
    Such a pilgrimage were sweet.
Yet do not; I would not go,
    Though at next door we might meet.
Though she were true when you met her,
And last till you write your letter,
            Yet she
            Will be
False, ere I come, to two or three.

This Donne poem calls for centering and for several indents best set by tabs. The next example of a table calls for columnar tab setting:

Table 3.7: The Characteristics of the J-402 Jet Engine and the F-107 Fan Engine Compared

	J-402	*F-107*
Length	*74 cm*	*79 cm*
Average diameter	*32 cm*	*31 cm*
Weight	*100 lbs*	*128 lbs*
Thrust (sea level static)	*600 lbs*	*860 lbs*
Specific fuel consumption		
(lb/hr/lb thrust)	*1.5*	*1*
Altitude flexibility	*Poor*	*Fair*
Exhaust temperature	*1,450° C*	*600° C*

If you computer has the capability of half-line spacing, the degree sign is made by using the lowercase letter "o" one half space up from the base line. Your software manual will point out whether your system has this capacity, and if so, how to use it. You must remember to instruct the system to return you to the base line immediately after the degree symbol or you will continue printing at the level of one-half space higher than your regular copy. If your system does not have the half-space capability, you'll probably have to put in the degree symbols by hand.

Try another table, one that might report the results of a questionnaire on salaries of personnel working for major newspapers:

Position	Average Salary	Average of Upper Quartile	Average Rise
Executive Editor (range £14.2–£55.0)	£32,500	£43,100	11.4%
Editor (range £10.0–£43.1)	£20,100	£30,100	12.3%
Senior Reporter (range £5.0–£34.0)	£15,000	£22,500	11.4%
Reporter (range £5.0–£22.5)	£14,400	£15,300	11.4%

9.2 FUNCTIONS

Further Cursor Movements

In all systems the cursors have the capability of moving forward and backward character by character and up and down line by line. Many also have the capability of moving forward and backward word by word, paragraph by paragraph, page by page, and from one end of the document to the other. Study your software manual to see how flexible your cursor movements are and train yourself to use the most convenient segment of movement for your purposes. The idea is to make the computer do as much work for you as possible. Use the single character movement when working within a word; the word movement when working within a line; the line movement when working within a paragraph; the paragraph movement when working within a page; and the page movement when working within larger document. Your program may also have the capability of going to a particular page. If you are working on a nine-page document and you want to make some changes on page 7, it is faster to "go to page 7" than it is to scroll forward from the beginning of page 1 or backward from the end of page 9.

Character Enhancement

Some systems also make "character enhancement" possible. Much here depends on the kind of printer you are using, as well as on the nature of your software and computer hardware. For instance, it is possible to print in a "compressed mode"—where the letters print smaller and closer together than normally.

A "double strike mode" allows you to overprint a character with a second printing of the same character to give a type of bolder appearance for emphasis. (It can also look messy, however, depending on the quality of your printer.)

You can use a "double width mode" that spreads your letters and spacing out to twice their normal widths.

And you can use "shadow printing" or an "emphasis mode" that prints the same letter twice, but in this one the second printing is just slightly to the side of the first printing.

You may even be able to combine these various modes to get a variety of options: double strike/double width/emphasis; double width/emphasis; double width/compressed; double strike/emphasis; double strike/compressed; and so on. Experiment with the various combinations to judge their appearances and their possible applications in your use of the computer. Normally they would be used for short subheadings (titles) of sections of a report or article. You can have a lot of fun playing with these mode combinations, but we recommend you do so on work you will keep for yourself. Use regular, straightforward printing on work you are preparing for others. They should concentrate on the content you want to communicate, rather than be distracted by a range of format peculiarities that take their attention away from your content.

10
New Keys: 67890^&*()

10.1 MORE NUMBERS AND SYMBOLS

In this chapter we introduce you to the last of the regular typing keys on the keyboard. These are the right-hand numbers and symbols. Familiarize yourself with them, beginning with the little finger and working in. Figure 18 shows these keys as they appear on your keyboard.

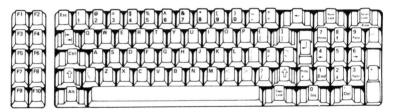

Figure 18

Move the little finger up beyond the "P" key to "0"; the third finger up beyond "O" to "9"; the second finger up beyond "I" to "8"; and the first finger up and beyond the "U" and "Y" keys to press both the "7" and "6" keys. The pattern is the same as for the left-hand fingers.

Try these examples:

09876 67890 090 080 070 060 909
989 979 969 808 898 878 868 707
797 787 767 606 696 686 676

And try these symbols:

() () () * & â

The parentheses are nearly always used in combination. The other symbols are used singly. The "¢" sign traditionally was the symbol used with the "6" key on American typewriters; it is no longer on a computer keyboard. It has been replaced by the "^" symbol. This symbol is used as part of the commands in many software programs. The ampersand ("&") is used primarily in names of companies. The US edition of this book is published by Doubleday & Company, Inc., for instance. The symbol is not generally used in formal writing any longer. The asterisk ("*") is useful in marking notes. These symbols, like some of those on the left-hand keys, were placed on typewriters at the turn of the century when these symbols were in much greater general use. Having been part of the standard keyboard for decades, it is almost automatic that they should be on a computer keyboard, even though one could imagine a number of other symbols that would be more useful at the dawn of the twenty-first century.

Dates

There are some combinations of numbers you will probably use with regularity. The first is the year. Try some:

1985 1985 1985 1985 1986 1986 1986 1987 1987

There are two styles of writing dates. One is the more traditional day/month/year; the other one, used by some foreign countries, has the order of month/day/year. Try some of each:

25 December 1985; 1 January 1986; 15 March 1985; 6 June 1945; 4 July 1776; 24 October 1492; 1 January 2000

And

December 25, 1985; January 1, 1986; March 15, 1985; June 6, 1945; July 4, 1776; October 24, 1492; January 1, 2000

The day/month/year combination has the advantage of omitting a comma, so if you use the style in a text, remember there are no commas;

On 25 April 1284 the first English Prince of Wales was born in Caernarvon town.

Whereas if you used the other style, there normally should be two commas:

On April 25, 1284, the first English Prince of Wales was born in Caernarvon town.

And in these days when keystrokes saved is money saved, the form that favours no commas is more widely used in business and publishing.

A third method of entering a date is very much dictated by computer capabilities. Government and business often want to sort and arrange data by date. The computer readily picks out and organizes numerical sequences, but far more complicated programs are needed for it to do the same for month/day/year sequences. So many forms now are prepared by year/month/day order, with the month and day always being expressed in two digits. January 1, 1987, becomes 19870101. December 25, 1950, becomes 195001225. By using this method your computer can sort from low to high (or high to low) numbers and thereby provide a chronological sequence in a single operation. Most of the people you relate to outside of government agencies and certain businesses would be confused if you used this method with them. But if you use dates as part of your own work with your computer, you might want to adopt this method for those limited purposes.

Because so many numbers are rounded out to the nearest ten or hundred, you will use the "0" key more than any other number key. Try:

In the 1800s England was still more rural than urban.
There must have been 100,000 people at the football final.
How long will it take me to get so I can do 50 pushups?

Here is a memo that uses numbers and symbols:

MEMORANDUM

19 August 1986

                    Purchasing Memorandum 86/58

From: Purchasing
To: Overseas Operations
Subject: Moving expenses

This is to establish new procedures regarding the payment of moving expenses for personnel transferred to overseas posts.

The company will pay for seven (7) cubic tons of household goods per family member. This amount can be aggregated per family unit, so a family unit of four (4) members qualifies for thirty-two (32) cubic tons of household goods. Any goods shipped in excess of the authorized allowance shall be done so at the transferee's personal expense, to be reimbursed to the company within thirty (30) days of the completion of the transfer.

Packing and pickup is authorized at the transferee's address of residence at the time of transfer. Overseas shipping is by sea for household goods and by air for immediate personal effects (not to exceed 300 pounds per family member). Delivery and unpacking is authorized at the transferee's home address in the overseas post.

The transferee is to secure three (3) bids from shippers listed in the *International Shippers Guide*. He may chose any of the three, provided the shipper chosen presents a bid that is no more than 8% higher than the lowest bid.

The transferee is allowed 3% of his annual salary as general relocation allowance. This is to cover such items as new curtains, carpets, and the like. No detailed accounting need be presented for this allowance, but it is to be taxed as regular income.

All food and board expenses, as well as travel costs, are paid by the company. Travel tickets may be purchased by the company in advance. Receipts shall be secured for all meals and lodging and are to be presented with an expense accounting for the trip to the overseas post. If a personal or family holiday is taken in conjunction with the trip to the overseas post, the company shall pay only for the cost of the most direct route of travel and reasonable meals and lodging that would have been incurred on such a route.

Travel expenses are to be submitted on Form 598/83/251. Shipping expenses are to be submitted on form 598/83/252.

Shipping bids are to be submitted to Purchasing with the indication of which shipper the transferee has elected to use at least six (6) weeks before the date of packing to enable Purchasing to prepare a purchase order for the shipper.

These procedures are effective as of 15 September 1986.*

John Wilts
Head, Purchasing Department
McGann & Co Ltd

* Any moves to overseas posts scheduled to occur before 1 January 1987
will follow the procedures set forth in Purchasing Memorandum 85/34.

You may want to prepare a price list. Here is a sample of a price list
for some restaurant costings. You would probably want some kind of
general description that would precede that actual price list. Try
this:

Example

A restaurant has a turnover in June of £3,000, and at this level of sales it
is necessary to make a gross profit of 61% of sales. Sales are divided into
three main types: meals, fruit, and sundries (the latter being ready-to-serve
foods such as bread rolls, butter pats in pre-packed portions, etc.). Menu
prices have been fixed to give different gross profit percentages on the
different types of sales. From the following information prepare a tabular
gross profit statement to show the gross profit percentage achieved for the
month in total and for each category.

		£
Stock at 1 June	Fresh fruit	2
	Sundries	11
	Other foodstuffs	82
Stock at 30 June	Fresh fruit	4
	Sundries	9
	Other foodstuffs	102
Purchases during June	Fresh fruit	92
	Sundries	193
	Other foodstuffs	900
Sales during June	Fresh fruit	200
	Sundries	400
	Meals	2,400

GROSS PROFIT STATEMENT FOR JUNE

	Total £	*Fruit* £	*Sundries* £	*Meals* £
Sales	3,000	200	400	2,400
Food cost:				
Stock at 1 June	95	2	11	82
Purchases	1,185	92	193	900

	1,280	94	204	982
Less Stock at 30 June	114	4	9	102
	1,165	90	195	880
Gross Profit	1,835	110	205	1,520
Gross profit %	61.1%	55.0%	51.2%	63.3%

It will be seen that with this sales mix a gross profit percentage of 63.3% on meals, 51.2% on sundries, and 55% on fruit produced an overall gross profit of 61.1% for the month. If the sales mix had been in different proportions the overall result would have been different. An example showing an extreme change in sales mix will demonstrate this more clearly:

Total sales £3,000, as above, made up of fruit £2,400, sundries £400, meals £200.

	Sales	*G.P.%*	*Gross profit*
Fruit	£2,400	55.0%	£1,320
Sundries	400	51.2%	205
Meals	200	63.3%	127
	3,000		1,652 = 55.1%

It is useful to have a list such as this on your computer. In another year, when the value of foods has risen, you need update only your prices. The format of the list remains the same.

Those who live in cities have always fantasized about the beauty and peace of being in the countryside. Back in about 1816, the twenty-one-year-old poet John Keats expressed in a short poem the feelings of many a city dweller. Try it with tabbed indents:

To One Who Has Been Long in City Pent

To one who has been long in city pent,
   'Tis very sweet to look into the fair
   And open face of heaven,—to breathe a prayer
   Full in the smile of the blue firmament.
Who is more happy, when, with heart's content,
   Fatigued he sinks into some pleasant lair

Of wavy grass, and reads a debonair
And gentle tale of love and languishment?
Returning home at evening, with an ear
Catching the notes of Philomel—and eye
Watching the sailing cloudlet's bright career,
He mourns that day so soon has glided by,
E'en like the passage of an angle's tear
That falls through the clear ether silently.

10.2 FUNCTIONS

Each software program has its own terminology for its menus. If you are using a word-processing program, you will become familiar soon enough with the primary functions and terms you need to do your basic typing. These are the functions discussed so far in this book. But there are additional functions (and terms) that are unique to your software and system. If you have a Tandy TRS-80, for instance, you can use any one of several word-processing programs, such as "Color Scripsit," "Telewriter 64," "Super Scripsit," "WordStar 3.0," and others. Your hardware (the TRS-80) is basically the same—you may need more memory and more disk drives with some programs—but the software gives you different functions and uses different terms to describe these functions.

Additional Commands

After you have become comfortable with the primary typing procedures, experiment from time to time with other functions that are displayed on the various menus in your program. The IBM PC/EasyWriter program offers a menu, for instance, called "Additional Commands." The following functions are possible from this menu:

Align Text; Centre a Line; HMI Setting; Justify On/Off; Margin Setting; Page of Copies; Print to Screen; Search and Replace; Tab Settings; Word Count; Go to Editor; Go to File System

Most of these functions are self-explanatory. But there are three or four that you have not used and you may wonder what they do. Use your manual to try them out. You will add functions to your capability that you may not need so far; but one of these days you'll want to do something, and one of those unused functions is just what's needed to make the job easy. If you hadn't experimented during some "play-with-the-system" time, you wouldn't know the function existed. It's not necessary to remember how to perform the function in detail; the menu will prompt you and the manual will always contain the details. It's necessary only to know the function is there and that you can get to it.

Horizontal Motion Index

As an example, you may want to know what the "HMI Setting" is. The manual index guides you to a short paragraph headed "Horizontal Motion Index" (HMI). You have no idea what the horizontal motion index is, so you read: "This special printer command does not function with the IBM 80 CPS Matrix Printer. If you have a non-IBM printer that uses HMI, see Appendix C." On that cryptic note, how can you not look up Appendix C? It says under "Horizontal Motion Index": "The Horizontal Motion Index (HMI) sets the amount of space that appears between each character. This command only works if you have a printer that is capable of movement in increments of 1/120 of an inch between characters. EasyWriter's default HMI is 11 (11 characters per inch)." With that information you think about your printer. If you have an IBM 80 CPS Matrix Printer, you can stop right now. But if you have an Okidata Microline 92 or a Mannesman Tally MT160L printer hooked up with your IBM PC system, then you may want to experiment with the HMI setting function to see what it can produce.

Word Count

Then you may want to find out about the "word count" function. The EasyWriter function passes the cursor through your document and counts the number of words in the document and gives the answer on the screen. In this software program, however, a "word" is any string of characters between two spaces. It will therefore include in its word count all the embedded commands you have entered to format your document. The reported word count will be slightly higher with EasyWriter than the actual word count—but still pretty close. This function is most useful if you write articles for a magazine, and the editor assigns you one of 850 words. Your word count function could be run occasionally as you proceed with the article, giving you a kind of running report on how to shape your article and when to start bringing it to a close.

Help Menu

Most programs have a help menu. Again, the contents and terminology will vary according to the specific software. The EasyWriter Help Menu serves as an example. It has the following functions:

Help On/Off; Insert Line; Delete Word; Stop Print; Align Marker; Print File(s); Add Commands; Undelete; Block Marker; File System; End-of-File; Delete Character; Top-of-Screen; Insert Mode On/Off; Delete to End-of-Line; Block Get; Block Put; Block Copy; Print Type; Top-of-File; Slow/Speed Print

These functions enable you to manipulate your copy on the screen or by printing it. And again, familiarize yourself with the various functions that are possible, even though you don't need them all now.

You may have started out with an inexpensive word-processing program that you thought would serve your needs. And in fact, it may. But more likely, you find that there are functions described in this book that your program cannot perform. The easiest answer might be to upgrade your system. This would involve getting a more sophisticated word-processing program that works on your computer. That program may require adding hardware components to the ones you already have. Look carefully at the cost of adding those components to your present investment and compare them with the cost of getting a new system with those components—and more—built in. The rate of innovation and price reduction is so great in this field that thought has to be given to the best way to upgrade capability.

11
Extra Keys

Nearly every computer keyboard has a few extra keys—beyond those already introduced in this book—for special application. On the IBM PC keyboard, these extra keys are: = + [ ] ¦ ¦ | \ ~ '. Figure 19 shows where they appear on the keyboard.

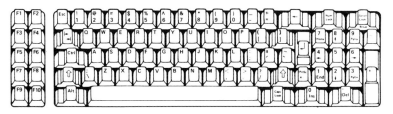

Figure 19

Apart from special applications, the keys you are most likely to use in the normal course of typing are the brackets ("[ ]") keys. Brackets are used to indicate parentheses within parentheses:

In the thirteenth century (called by some [not me] the Greatest of All Centuries), learning and questioning was equalled only by the fervour of the Inquisition.

Other Extra Keys

The other extra keys are more generally used in association with a computer program. Since they are not a part of regular typing, we suggest you use them as you need them and look for them at those times. When pressing them, use whichever finger feels most comfortable. You'll be so used to using your little fingers in regular typing, that use of the little finger for these keys will seem normal, especially when you watch what you are doing.

The "~" symbol can be used in scientific, mathematical, or statistical copy to mean "difference."

The vertical line ("¶") and vertical broken line ("¦) symbols are used in creating vertical lines like those of a box or parts of a table or chart in the presentation of data.

The backward slash ("\") can be used in chemical copy to mean "single bond," as can the vertical line ("¶").

The "+" symbol is used to indicate addition or "plus," the "=" symbol to indicate "equal to." If you use a strikeover combination, "≠" indicates "not equal to" and "≢" indicates "not identical with."

A combination hyphen and colon appears as "÷" and indicates "divided by." And the hyphen followed by the colon ("-:") indicates "difference excess."

If the plus sign is underlined in a combination character ("±"), it indicates "plus or minus."

The majority of these symbols are used only in technical work—mathematics, science, statistics—and do not occur in general typing. However, it is sometimes useful to know that your computer can produce them if they are needed.

Other combination characters that may come into use occasionally are the cedilla: a combination of "c" and "," ("ç"); the yen symbol: a combination of "Y" and "=" ("¥"); and the umlaut: a combination of a vowel with a "″" ("ö" or "ü" or "ä"). None of these combination characters is entirely satisfactory, but they can serve, if needed. If you need regular use of them, you would be better off getting a software/printer/printwheel combination that has these characters on them. Language programs, with all the appropriate accent marks, are readily available to use on the computer system.

11.1 FUNCTIONS

Filing and Recall

Apart from managing the entering of letters and commands that make up the content and format or shape of your document, you need to familiarize yourself with the capabilities and methods your system has for filing and recalling your document. Your software manual will describe how to create a "file," giving it a specific name so you can have access to it in the future by use of that name. A file is a body of data under a single name that is stored on a disk. The file is your document with all its letters and commands.

Once you create a file, you need to know how to revise it, that is, change, add, and delete both words and commands from time to time according to your use of the file. You need to know how to store or file it on a disk and call it up again. On some systems, you have to file an entire document at once; on other systems, you can file part of a document as you continue to work on the rest of it. This last option is the better one, if you can use it. The danger point in losing data in a computer is between the time you create and enter the data and the time you store it on a disk. If you can continue to store parts of the document as you work through it, the amount of the data you might lose from a power failure is minimal. If you cannot store data part by part, you should end or file your document every couple of pages and then call it up again to your screen for continued revision as you carry on completing your work. This is a bother and is time-consuming, but it is better than unexpectedly losing your entire document before you have a chance to store it. Whatever you store is at least on a disk.

Block Move

Sometimes you will want to move part of your document into the body of another document, either because it fits better there or because you want to repeat information at another place. You therefore have to learn how to move blocks of text from one file to another, from one disk to another. Here again you must experiment with the instructions in your software manual on file management.

Other File Functions

The various file functions you need to master in order to do what you want with ease with your copy are (your system may use different titles for these functions, but they will be part of your file management program): add or append a file to one already in existence; delete an entire file; edit or revise a file; get a file; link more than one file together or link them so the same operation takes place in more than one file; display the index or catalogue of a diskette; save (or file) a file; print a file; and stop print of a file. The term "file" (as a noun) means the same as "document"; the term "file" as a verb means to store the document or file onto a disk.

Knowing how to type your words and commands, how to manage your files or documents, how to set up your commands and margins, and how to print out your document gives you mastery of your computer. Gaining this mastery is enjoyable, a challenge met. What you enter into your computer—as data and as words—is the real test of the computer's usefulness to you. We wish you good typing, of course! But even more, we hope that your computer will be more productive than ever in the tasks it accomplishes for you because you can use its keyboard with greater ease, fewer errors, and enhanced speed.

12
Some Other Keyboards

The IBM Personal Computer is not the only personal computer on the market, of course. We have chosen it as our model because of its leading position in the personal computer market, but we are fully aware of other systems that sell widely.

Rather than try to illustrate every possible keyboard in a rapidly changing field, we have selected a few samples of other popular computers. We will show how they differ from the IBM PC keyboard in such a way that you can readily compare these keyboards with your own.

A popular system is the COMPAQ™ Computer. This is a low-priced, portable computer that has chosen to be as fully compatible with the IBM PC as possible. In fact, the keyboard is a duplicate of the IBM PC keyboard.

Another popular portable computer is the ACT Apricot. The Apricot keyboard is shown as Figure 20. Note the following features about this keyboard:

Figure 20

● The four cursor keys are at the top right of the keyboard keys. They are dedicated to cursor use, unlike the IBM PC keyboard where the cursor keys are in the ten-key number pad and used when the number lock mode is off.

• The Apricot ten-key number pad is dedicated to numbers. It has its own enter or return key in addition to the return key at the right of the regular typing keyboard.

• The letters, numbers, symbols, escape, tab, control, caps lock, shift, and space bars are standard. Note that the caps lock key is situated just above the left-hand shift key; this is similar to many typewriter locations.

The Tandy TRS-80 Computer comes in several models. The keyboard shown as Figure 21 is basic to them all. On later models

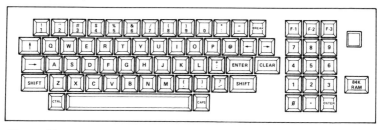

Figure 21

there may be one or two more function keys or dedicated keys added, but this figure adequately represents the TRS-80 family of computer keyboards. Note the following features of this keyboard:

• There are three function keys located above the ten-key number pad.

• The cursor keys are located at either end of the regular typing keyboard. The left and right cursor keys are to the right of the "P" key; the up and down cursor keys are to the left of the "Q" and "A" keys.

• The colon (":") is on the top line to the right of the "0" key.

• The plus symbol ("+") is in the shift mode of the semicolon (";").

• The parentheses have been moved over one key each to the left: The open parenthesis ("(") is the shift mode of the "8" key; the close parenthesis (")") is the shift mode of the "9" key.

• There is no symbol in the shift mode of the "0" key.

• The asterisk ("*") is in the shift mode of the colon (":") key.

• The apostrophe, single quotation mark, minute, and foot symbol ("'") is in the shift mode of the "7" key.

• The double quotation mark, second, and inch symbol ('"') is in the shift mode of the "2" key.

• The "at" symbol ("@") has its own key immediately to the right of the "P" key.

• The hyphen is two keys to the right of the "0" key, and the equals symbol ("=") is in the shift mode of that key.

• The caps lock key is to the immediate right of the space bar; the control key to the immediate left of the space bar.

• Two keys, called "break" and "clear" serve functional purposes described in the software manuals.

• There is a separate enter or return key for the ten-key number pad.

• There is no delete or backspace key.

• The letter keys and numbers are arranged in the normal QWERTY pattern.

The Apple IIe computer is very popular. Figure 22 shows the keyboard.

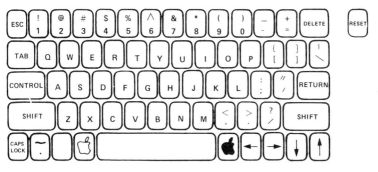

Figure 22

Note the following features about this keyboard:

• There is a symbol key immediately to the right of the "brackets and braces" key:

• The caps lock key is in the lower left corner of the keyboard.

• The following key is to the right of the caps lock key: ~

• The four cursor keys are in a row at the lower right-hand corner of the keyboard.

• The "open Apple," "solid Apple," and "reset" keys are used as function keys; these functions are described in the software manuals.

• The letters, numbers, and symbols are arranged in the standard QWERTY pattern, as are the escape, tab, shift, backspace (or delete), and return keys and the space bar.

Digital Equipment Corporation (DEC) has a number of microcomputers that share the same keyboard. The personal computer is marketed under the name "Rainbow." Figure 23 shows the Rainbow keyboard.

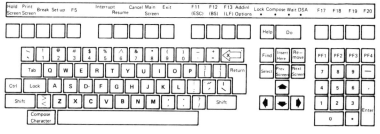

Figure 23

Note the following features about this keyboard:

● There are 105 keys on this keyboard, grouped in four main areas. These groupings are: (1) the main QWERTY typing keyboard; (2) the ten-key number pad; (3) the editing keypad, located between the QWERTY grouping and the ten-key number pad; and (4) the special function keys, located along the top of the keyboard above the other three groupings.

● The special function keys are programmable by the various software programs loaded into the system. With each software program comes a plastic strip that fits just above these keys and gives a short description of the function served by each key in that particular software program. There are eighteen such programmable keys on the keyboard, plus four lights that provide messages to you when they light up.

● The ten-key number pad has its own enter or return key. This grouping also has four programmable keys, located in the line above the ten-key number pad. In addition, each of the keys in this pad can serve other functions, depending on the software program.

● The four cursor keys are located at the bottom of the "screen/cursor control" grouping.

● There are eight keys in the "screen/cursor control" grouping that are dedicated to basic command functions. Rather than having to enter the entire command and then execute it by pressing the return or enter key, a single press on one of these keys will enter the command into the system and call for its execution. Detailed use of the keys is described in each software manual.

● The "compose character" key is immediately to the left of the space bar. It is normally used only in advanced software applications with computer systems that have more power than the personal computer.

● The comma and full stop characters are entered by those keys in both the regular and the shift mode.

● The "vee" brackets are on a single key, located between the "Z" and the left-hand shift key.

● The ~ key is located to the immediate left of the "1" key.

● The backspace or delete key is marked by a small "x" in a block arrow that points to the left. Its position is standard.

● The letters, numbers, and symbols are all arranged in the standard QWERTY pattern, as are the tab, caps lock, shift, backspace, and return keys and the space bar.

With minimum orientation to the keys on any computer, you can now readily find your way around the keyboard and use it with ease. However they are physically arranged, keys serve the following main purposes in computer use: (1) typing in words and commands (the QWERTY area); (2) entering numbers and arithmetical commands (the ten-key number pad, if there is one); (3) screen/cursor control (with greater or fewer numbers of dedicated keys for these purposes); and (4) programmable function keys (usually found only in the more expensive personal computers in any number). By analyzing any keyboard you sit before with these categories in mind, you will soon feel comfortable in getting that keyboard to make the system do the job you want done.

There is one final feature that must be mentioned at this time. Hewlett-Packard has a computer that uses light beams near the screen as an "enter" device. There are several light beams that crisscross the screen and provide a number of combinations that can send different electronic signals to the computer when the light is broken in these different locations on the screen. Figure 24 illustrates this in a simple diagram.

If for instance, the 3/D light combination is broken, a different electronic signal is generated than when a 2/B or 1/A combination is broken. In this example, there are twelve possible combinations.

The software provides menu options by placing pictures, graphics, numbers, or letters on the screen under the location of the crisscross light combinations. You are then asked to make your choice by touching the screen where the picture or letter or number is located. What you do really is break the light, which in turn generates the command that executes that option on the menu.

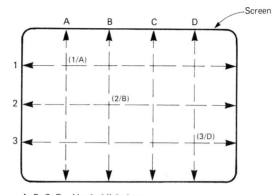

A, B, C, D = Vertical light beams
1, 2, 3 = Horizontal light beams

Figure 24

Whether this will become a standard feature in the future is far too early to tell. Whether it is even clearer or easier than relying solely on keys is also too early to tell. It, in effect, gives you programmable functional "keys" in the form of light beams just immediately in front of your screen surface. Instead of slipping a plastic sheet or a template near your functional keys—as is done on a regular keyboard—the system tells you what functions the light beam combinations serve by screen graphics. "A key by any other name is still a key," even though it's called "touch the screen."

12.1 THE DVORAK KEYBOARD

The QWERTY keyboard was developed in about 1873 by Christopher Latham Sholes for an early typewriter manufactured by the Remington Arms company. The typewriter was a primitive affair compared to electronic typewriters and word processors in use today. (See Figure 25.) The keys were operated by forceful manual striking, engaging a series of levers and wires. When the type bar hit the platen, it returned to its home position by gravity. The entire effort of typing was cumbersome and slow.

Mr. Sholes designed a keyboard that presumed most people would "hunt and peck" with their first fingers. He also deliberately placed keys that were used often in locations that would allow time for gravity

Figure 25

to return the type bars, so that there would be as little jamming of the bars at the impact point as possible. His keyboard—now called the QWERTY keyboard—was excellently designed for that early typewriter but is hardly the best for today's high-speed equipment. However, the QWERTY keyboard was early adopted as the standard keyboard for typewriters, and it has become the worldwide standard arrangement.

Typing studies done in the 1930s and 1940s showed that typists most frequently misspelled the following words in this order or error frequency:

the, to, of, and, is, which, it, that, when, for, with, here, and be

These single-syllable words are very common; the reason for a high frequency of error was surely not a lack of knowing how to spell them or a lack of occasion to use them. Time and motion studies were undertaken and revealed the following catalogue of weaknesses inherent in the QWERTY keyboard arrangement:

1. The QWERTY keyboard overloads the usually weaker left hand. The characters normally struck by the fingers of the left hand account for about 57 per cent of normal copy; leaving only 43 per cent for the fingers of the more usually skilful right hand. Left-handed people would find this arrangement a positive factor. This overloading of the generally weaker hand creates the need for concentration and, therefore, contributes to operator fatigue.

2. The QWERTY keyboard was originally designed for two-finger typing, and therefore it assigned too much work for the first fingers in comparison with the work done by the other fingers.

3. On the QWERTY keyboard only 32 per cent of normal typing is done with the keys of the home row. Sixty-eight per cent is done with the keys of the row above the home row; and 16 per cent with the keys of the row below the home row. It has been estimated that not more than about 100 words (including plurals using "s" and verbs that end with "s") can be typed with only the home row keys. For most words, therefore, the fingers must reach up and down. In many cases, they must jump over the home row altogether:

   December, expect, extreme, nerve, minimum, monocyte

   This unnecessary reaching increases time, energy, and concentration.

4. The QWERTY keyboard demands an unusual amount of finger jumping—going from row to row in immediate succession—in typing words that are used often in English. These finger-jumping letter combinations include:

   br, ce, ec, ny, my, um, nu, mi, ni, im, in, om, on, mo, no, and so on

5. The arrangement of the QWERTY keyboard requires thousands of words to be typed by the fingers of the left (usually the weaker) hand alone. The stronger and more agile right hand just waits while this left-hand activity goes on. Such words include:

   extra, address, was, saw, were, tree, free, freed, frees, crease, freeze, and so on

   In like manner, there are many words that use only the fingers of the right hand:

   hoop, pool, ply, kill, hill, lull, mull, you, loop, mop, nip, monopoly, July, ploy

If you sometimes have wondered why touch typing has been difficult to just pick up, the fault lies more with the QWERTY keyboard than with any innate problem of neuromuscular coordination. Various people have tried to design a simplified keyboard to replace the QWERTY keyboard. Every effort met with initial interest but ultimate failure because so many typists had already learned to type on the QWERTY keyboard and typewriter manufacturers had already made millions of typewriters with QWERTY keyboards. The cost of retraining typists was deemed too great for any change to be introduced.

August Dvorak, a pioneer in conducting American time and motion studies of typing, was eventually named director of the Carnegie Foundation for the Advancement of Teaching Study of Typewriting. He developed and patented a simplified keyboard that resolved most of the problems of the QWERTY keyboard. Now called the Dvorak keyboard, this simplified keyboard has the following features:

1. The right hand does more work on the Dvorak keyboard—56 per cent of the work in normal typing; leaving the left hand to do only 44 per cent.
2. On the Dvorak keyboard the work assigned to the various fingers is appropriate to their skill, strength and length.
3. On the Dvorak keyboard 70 per cent of the typing is done with keys on the home row! Only 22 per cent is done on the row above the home row; and a mere 8 per cent on the row below.
4. Finger motions from row to row have been greatly reduced—by nearly 90 per cent! In QWERTY typing, the fingers of a full-time typist with a high typing speed (100 words per minute) during an eight-hour day will move approximately sixteen miles. On a Dvorak keyboard, for the same typist doing the same work in the same amount of time the fingers will move only one mile.
5. More than 3,000 words—35 per cent of all the words used in normal copy—are typed exclusively on the keys of the home row.
6. Whereas on the QWERTY keyboard nearly 4,000 words are typed with the fingers of one hand alone, only sixty-one infrequently used monosyllabic words are so typed on the Dvorak keyboard.
7. The Dvorak keyboard places all five English vowels as left-hand home row keys and the most constantly used consonants as right-hand home row keys. This calls for alternating right-hand and left-hand fingering, which is a much faster and more accurate sequencing than confining many of these moves to the fingers of one hand.

Even though numerous tests and studies over four decades have shown that use of the Dvorak keyboard results in less fatigue, fewer errors, and greater efficiency, neither industry nor governments have embraced a change from the QWERTY keyboard. Industry and governments have both been fearful that retraining costs would be too great. The most dramatic test was conducted in 1944 by the U.S. Navy. Fourteen QWERTY typists were retrained for an average of eighty-three hours each to use the Dvorak keyboard, and a control group of eighteen QWERTY typists were given an average of 158 hours each of QWERTY upgrade training. The results showed the Dvorak trainees increased their output as measured in speed and accuracy by 74 per cent, as against a 43 per cent increase by the upgraded QWERTY typists who received twice as much training. The American Navy ordered 2,000 Dvorak keyboards, only to be turned down by a more conservative government purchasing office.

Dvorak developed his keyboard on a careful analysis of how English is used, as well as on a time and motion basis. He found, for instance, that one half of all written English consists of only sixty-nine words—ones that are used over and over again. And even more surprising, four-fifths of normal written English is composed of a mere 640 words. He was very careful, therefore, to ensure that these words were easily reached with the simplest of finger combinations possible.

In 1982, the Dvorak keyboard was approved by The American National Standards Institute, Inc. (ANSI) as an alternative keyboard to the long-lived QWERTY keyboard. ANSI has issued a specification book for the Dvorak keyboard to guide manufacturers who wish to include it as an option. Figure 26 is a reproduction of the Dvorak keyboard as adapted to an Apple IIe keyboard configuration.

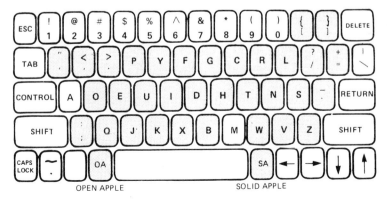

Figure 26

Although few typewriter manufacturers are going to drop the QWERTY keyboard in favour of the Dvorak keyboard, if only because the marketplace accepts such changes very slowly, many computer manufacturers offer the Dvorak keyboard as a readily obtainable alternative. Among them are IBM, DEC, Wang, Hewlett-Packard, Apple, Key Tronics (for the IMB PC), and others. There are also conversion kits that can be easily secured that will convert your Tandy, Apple, Texas Instrument, Commodore, and other personal computer keyboards to Dvorak use.

An option you should consider as you approach learning to touch-type on a computer keyboard is to use the Dvorak keyboard rather than your standard-issue QWERTY keyboard. You should probably do this only if you will be the prime user of the keyboard. If you are going to share the keyboard with others who already use the QWERTY pattern, they will have to hunt and peck on the Dvorak. However, as you are entering into the whole new world of computer use—with your own personal computer and with all the newness this embodies both in using the state of the art and in developing new skills for yourself—you might enjoy going all out and using the "new" keyboard as well. You have little to unlearn; and learning the Dvorak keyboard involves fewer awkward keystrokes by far than the QWERTY requires. Being a Dvorak typist on your personal computer puts you in a very select group. Most people won't even know what you are talking about when you tell them, even though your typing is far easier and more efficient.

Index